TWISTING THE TRUTH

TWISTING THE TRUTH

BRUCE TUCKER

BETHANY HOUSE PUBLISHERS
MINNEAPOLIS, MINNESOTA 55438
A Division of Bethany Fellowship, Inc.

Published by Bethany House Publishers
A Division of Bethany Fellowship, Inc.
6820 Auto Club Road, Minneapolis, Minnesota 55438

Printed in the United States of America

Library of Congress Cataloging-in-Publication Data

Tucker, Bruce, 1951-
   Twisting the truth.

   Includes bibliographies.
   1. Cults—Controversial literature.   2. Sects—Controversial literature.   3. Theology, Doctrinal—Popular works.   I. Title.
BP603.T82   1987   291   87-740
ISBN 0-87123-931-0 (pbk.)

Dedication

To Margie, my wife,
who typed, retyped, checked,
or corrected much of the material
for the manuscript.

To Chris, Phil, and Jeni,
my children, who are
my pride and great joy.

To the Lord Jesus Christ,
who not only provides life eternal,
but life abundant.

BRUCE TUCKER received a B.A. from Marshall University and a M.Div. at Trinity Evangelical Divinity School. He lectured for a number of years on apologetics as a staff member of Campus Crusade for Christ and developed a teaching curriculum on apologetics. He also lectured and debated at several universities on this issue. He is presently the pastor of the University Baptist Church in Gainesville, Florida.

Contents

◆ ◆

Why Study the Cults?

In our culture the basis of life is "live and let live." Therefore, the question frequently surfaces as to why we even study the cults. If their particular religious convictions vary from ours and they are happy, why challenge them? Many believe that absolute truth does not exist. All is relative. Truth is what is true for you. Combine this attitude with the popular mind-set that takes care of Number One first and truth becomes simply that which makes you happy.

For Christians, this mind-set is an unacceptable alternative. We believe in absolutes, understand that truth is knowable, and that the Scriptures are truth. What we believe and how we live are important. Eternal destinies are at stake. Consequently, we must understand the biblical perspective, submitting our feelings, experience, and circumstances to God's truth.

In this light, the study of cults takes on great importance. The church has the responsibility of guarding her sheep from being scattered and of evangelizing the lost. Cults pose a challenge to both of these purposes.

The church is vulnerable. Many in the church know what they believe but have no conviction as to why. Christians are too often easily misled. Eighty percent of cultists come from Christian churches.[1] We must be better equipped when confronted by cults.

Christians are responsible to study God's Word. We are commanded to discern truth from error (1 John 4:1–6) and to be students of Scripture (2 Tim. 3:13–17). Paul also warns that there are serious implications when we do not learn discernment.

---

[1]Walter Martin, *Introduction to the Cults*, cassette tape by One Way Library.

> I am astonished that you are so quickly deserting the one who
> called you by the grace of Christ and are turning to a different
> gospel—which is really no gospel at all. Evidently some people
> are throwing you into confusion and are trying to pervert the
> gospel of Christ. But even if we or an angel from heaven should
> preach a gospel other than the one we preached to you, let him
> be eternally condemned. (Gal. 1:6–8)

Cultic theology is a distortion of biblical truth. Admittedly,
studying the Bible always opens the door to the possibility of
misunderstanding it. But if we study the Bible, we should learn
from historic cultic errors. It is important that the church understand the true Christian position. The stakes are too high to
ignore it. Many of the leaders at Jonestown, Guyana, had been
Sunday school teachers before joining Jim Jones.

Today we are encountering an even more significant problem. Cults are being accepted enthusiastically into the church,
and large sectors of Christianity are adhering to cultic theologies
and practices. A denomination that claims to be one of the fastest
growing groups in the country has followers of several distinct
cultic groups as members in good standing and has recruited
leaders of those cults to teach seminars at its annual convention.
The organization has even encouraged its affiliated churches to
adopt some of the practices and principles of these cults. The
president of this "post-denominational" council has maintained
that the beliefs of Gnosticism and pantheism characterize the
true heart of the council.

How have people responded? The council is growing! This
may be due to the fact that Christians are either unaware of the
direction of the council, or have been falsely discipled for so long
that they are not able to discern this drastic error! After years of
laying the foundation and setting the girders in place, the bricks
now being laid can only fit the scheme of the design.

It is a sad commentary on the condition of the church when
large groups accept the beliefs and practices of recognized cults
(and even the occult) without reservations, and express indig-
nation at those who would challenge this practice.

The church not only has the responsibility to protect its members, but also to reach out to those who do not know the gospel.
Peter wrote the classic text for cultic apologetics: "But in your

hearts set apart Christ as Lord. Always be prepared to give an answer to everyone who asks you to give the reason for the hope that you have. But do this with gentleness and respect" (1 Pet. 3:15).

On the basis of our love for Christ, we should be prepared to evangelize anyone, at anytime, anywhere. We are to witness in a reverent and loving way, approaching people not as enemies to be conquered but as people for whom Christ died.

The admonition to "contend earnestly for the faith" (Jude 3, NASB) is still true today. Therefore, we should be especially concerned that cultic influence is growing. One hundred fifty years ago there were approximately one thousand cultists in the United States.[2] In 1980 there were approximately twenty million cultists and approximately 2,000 different groups.[3]

While we all make errors in our interpretation of Scripture from time to time, the organized proclamation of another gospel is the fault of the father of lies. However, cultists are blinded by the devil (1 Tim 4:1) and are not the devil himself. Blind people need to be enlightened with the light of the gospel, not ridiculed and persecuted.

A thorough knowledge of the truth will help protect us from the false. As we understand truth and obey it, it will conform us more to Christ's image and help us develop a sound Christian life.

---

[2]Walter Martin, ibid.
[3]Bob Larson, *Larson's Book of Cults* (Wheaton, Ill.: Tyndale House Publishers, 1982), p. 19.

A Cure for Doctrine-Phobia

Your next-door neighbors have never attended church very regularly. They do not pretend to be religious or claim to know much about the Bible. However, their teenage daughter has been asked by a small group of religious people to attend a weekend retreat on a farm they have purchased outside of town. These people have been evangelizing the youth in your community and starting special Bible studies. With all the headlines about cults, your neighbors are asking you about that group. Since you attend church, they feel that you can answer their questions.

Another religious group has started renting a large room at the local bank. They have been going door to door, witnessing and starting evening Bible studies in several homes. The name of the fellowship is unfamiliar, not that of a known denomination. Could they be a cult?

Your oldest son has arrived home during Christmas break from college. Although you raised him in the church, he seems to have gained a *new* enthusiasm for God. This pleases you, but there are some negative results. He is condemning your church. He tends to criticize the practices of the traditional church; he even has doubts about your faith. Has he gotten involved in a cult while at college?

Each of these scenarios could involve cults or true Christian groups. I know of examples similar to these on both sides. You're probably asking, "How can I tell if a group is a cult?" If it is not large and is not already referred to in one of the major works on cults, you may not know with confidence. There are over 2,000 cultic groups in the United States and only a very few have been written about by the experts.

As your neighbors persist in asking you whether their daughter should attend the retreat, you feel uncomfortable about what to say. If the group is a Christian fellowship, you are glad that she is so interested. However, if they are not, you recognize the dangers of cultic involvement.

How can you tell? Usually, the first thing you ask is the name of the group. Second, you often ask, "How do they conduct themselves? What do they do? Do they live as Christians should?" But at some point the crucial question is asked, "What do they believe and teach?"

In answering this question, you will have the greatest opportunity to discern if the group is, or is not, a cult.

Why a Doctrinal Book?

The market seems flooded with books about cults. The majority of them investigate either one group very thoroughly, or several groups in a brief, survey fashion. Some books attempt to study the cults from a unique angle, such as their particular doctrinal errors. But why write a book solely from a doctrinal perspective?

An individual who has done only a brief study of cults quickly sees that the number of different groups in the United States is very large. Some estimate that there are 1,500 to 3,000 different cults.[1] Some estimate that the number of people involved in cults and the occult in the United States alone approaches twenty million.

Some of the fastest growing religious organizations are actually cults. Fortunately, these larger groups, such as the Mormons and Jehovah's Witnesses, are well identified, thoroughly researched, and widely written about.

Unfortunately, in many of the texts, true Christian doctrine is often lost in the mass of information about the unique beliefs of cults. Typically, books on cults tend to focus on the teachings

---

[1]Bob Larson, *Larson's Book of Cults* (Wheaton, Ill: Tyndale House Publishers, 1982), p. 19.

of a few of the groups and add Christian doctrine on the side. This at best creates experts on Mormonism, Jehovah's Witnesses, and Christian Scientists; at worst it produces individuals mixed up as to which group believes what. On the average, though, the information produces individuals who recognize the major groups as cults and know some interesting trivia on each.

But the vast majority of groups have not been identified. The average layman is not sure whether a group is cultic if it is not included in one of the major books on cults. Therefore, today, as in the past, the best approach to the cults is a solid understanding of what true Christian doctrine is and why we adhere to it.

The Christian needs to know which doctrines are key in separating true Christianity from false Christianity, which views in those doctrines are proper, and why the believer can claim the proper interpretation. All these issues need to be addressed to adequately ground the Christian in the faith.

I am amazed at how many small fellowships, some even nestled quietly away in small towns and rural areas, are espousing cultic positions and practices. With this vast number of cults in the United States, no one will ever be able to cover all the groups. But we can cover Christianity and demonstrate the typical ways cults will twist the truth.

The need for a doctrinal perspective is further reinforced by the fact that there are vast differences between many of the groups. Most who have studied the cults have quickly discerned how difficult it is to define a cult or a cult member. There is a world of difference between a black-tied Mormon missionary and a saffron-robed Hare Krishna devotee.

Some attempt to define cults by emphasizing sociological characteristics. For example, extreme loyalty to an individual, the development of similar habit patterns, jargon, appearance, and very active fund raising are common marks of cults.

These characteristics can be helpful, but sociological characteristics may be too subjective. How much loyalty by how many people would qualify a group as a cult? Can Christians be loyal to a leader? Is it wrong to be loyal? How prevalent and unique must the jargon be? Girl Scouts are even known to dress alike, use some similar terminology, and peddle chocolate mint cookies quite effectively. It is possible, and it has occurred in the past, that Christian groups have been classified as cults because of the misapplication of those sociological characteristics. The less subjective the criteria is, the better.

Fortunately, the church has a less subjective basis for discerning cults: the Bible. Scripture helps us to identify those doctrines, individuals, and groups which cannot be a part of the true body of Christ. In fact, many of the New Testament epistles deal specifically with helping Christians discern false teachers, twisted doctrines, and heretical groups. Peter warns us about those who "distort the Scriptures to their own destruction" (2 Pet. 3:16). John gives a doctrinal test to help the church to determine those who are of God, "Every spirit that acknowledges that Jesus Christ has come in the flesh is from God" (1 John 4:2).

Paul frequently emphasized the importance of maintaining sound doctrine. In Second Timothy, after discussing the authority and inspiration of Scripture, he concludes with this charge:

> Preach the Word; be prepared in season and out of season; correct, rebuke and encourage—with great patience and careful instruction. For the time will come when men will not put up with sound doctrine. Instead, to suit their own desires, they will gather around them a great number of teachers to say what their itching ears want to hear. They will turn their ears away from the truth and turn aside to myths. (2 Tim. 4:2–4)

Elsewhere, Paul speaks of those who, because of false doctrine, receive another Jesus, another gospel, and another spirit (2 Cor. 11:4).

When a prophet speaks of Jesus, to whom does he or she refer, the Jesus of the Bible or another Jesus? What is the prophet's gospel? Is it the same salvation taught in the Bible or a different way? Is it personal merit or works? Scripture's position is nonnegotiable on these matters. This book will define some of those specific doctrines and demonstrate the ways in which cults twist them.

Objections to a Doctrinal Book

Who chooses the doctrine?

If the Jews were writing this book in the first century, the Christians would be defined as cultic. If the Roman Catholics were writing this book in the sixteenth century, the followers of Luther, Calvin, and Zwingli would be defined as cultists. For that matter, if Luther, Calvin, and Zwingli were writing this book, they might have called each other cultists. Who has the right to determine the doctrinal criteria?

All philosophies and views are based upon certain presuppositions. I believe we have inerrant revelation from God in the Scriptures and that there is both internal and external evidence to lend support to that foundation. The authors of the Bible defined certain issues as being extremely important. We will let them speak.

Which doctrines should we use as criteria?

Naturally, the Bible teaches a vast number of doctrines. Some doctrines are more important than others. This is apparent even in the fact that the Holy Spirit apparently inspired the authors to make some doctrines clearer than others. The apostles admonished the church to love and accept each other in spite of differences in those gray areas.

However, some doctrines are unambiguously clear. Apostolic admonitions state clearly that errors on those issues are heresy. In Galatians Paul warns that the teacher of a false gospel should be "eternally condemned" (Gal. 1:8). John teaches that those who deny the proper identity of Jesus are antichrists.

Once when a Christian friend of mine was talking about the importance of these doctrinal criteria, he mentioned his concern that emphasizing such doctrinal issues would surely cause division in the body of Christ. However, these doctrines are not a long list of issues which Christians often debate. We must be careful that we do not become so concerned about harmony and unity that we compromise nonnegotiables of the faith and find ourselves in fellowship with the kingdom of the cults. While Christians can and do differ on eschatology, there is no room for flexibility on issues like the gospel or the person of Jesus Christ.

How can these doctrines be the basis for orthodoxy when the early church had not even fully defined them?

It is true that the nature of Christ was not clearly stated in a creed until the Council of Nicea in A.D. 325. It is also true that justification by faith was debated in the early church. Yes, even the books of the New Testament were not itemized until after a conflict with Marcion and the development of his incomplete canon. How can we call a group *unorthodox* today when the early church had not defined orthodoxy for itself?

Just because the early church wrestled with truth, as we do now, does not mean that truth is not discernible. The question is, "What is the source of truth?" The apostles received revelation. Even though a canon of Scripture had not been tested, their words and writings were considered as authoritative as the Old Testament writings. *Orthodoxy* was defined in their writings. The councils, attempting to define orthodoxy after the deaths of the apostles, appealed to apostolic authority and the Scriptures. The listing of the canon was simply the recognition of an established group of authoritative writings.

The fact that the early church wrestled with the meaning of the Scripture, as we do today, does not deny the existence of the authority of the apostles or their writings, nor does it imply that the meaning of the gospel changes with each new generation. The basis for truth is not the early church in and of itself, but the apostolic authority to write Scripture. Creeds are not revelation, nor was truth absent before the creeds were penned. The creeds were the church's catalog of what it believed the Scriptures taught.

The early church was not free from debate on doctrinal issues. The Book of Acts and several epistles refer to such debates. However, authoritative conclusions were reached. As we study the Scripture, we learn what those conclusions were, and use them as the basis of orthodoxy.

How can these doctrines be good criteria when they also imply that other "religions" are actually "cults"?

Recall again, first of all, that the term "cult" is difficult to define. Many groups classified as cults today are forms of Eastern philosophy and Hinduism. It is true that these groups are not "cults" in the usual sense, but small Hindu sects.

To answer our question, we need to review some history. The earliest American "cults" were categorized as psuedo-Christian.

They usually claimed to be the true Christian Church restored after a period of apostasy and decadence. They usually claimed the Bible, to some degree, as their authority. For most of what we may call earlier cult history, since the nineteenth century, these groups were considered cults by people who studied them. As they were studied, often in relationship to their doctrine, it was discovered that these groups generally deviated consistently in specific doctrinal areas. Hence, today we have the doctrinal criteria.

However, more recent cultic history has included the influx of Eastern theologies and other small groups. They are not psuedo-Christian, do not claim to be the true Christian Church, or even care to appear Christian. They are generally small Hindu sects. Realistically then, they represent Hinduism and an entirely different world view: monism.

However, our culture adapted the term "cult" and applied it to these Eastern groups principally for sociological reasons. Nevertheless, it is also true that they do not adhere to the same doctrinal positions as the church, not because they are attempting to deviate from Christianity, but because their roots are in Hinduism.

The door has been opened to judge other religions by the doctrines which define psuedo-Christian cults. It is not that the doctrinal criteria were developed to include other religions, but that the ways in which psuedo-Christian cults deviate from Christianity can also be found in other religions.

Can these doctrinal criteria be effective if they sometimes apply to some present traditional denominational churches?

Some churches have denied certain doctrinal criteria we will use to define cults. This is the result of the changing authority ascribed to Scripture. As the authority of Scripture is compromised, so follow very important doctrinal truths. Certainly I would be hesitant to call these groups cults.

But the reason that the early church chose these cultic criteria was a general warning for everyone. These doctrinal criteria were later applied to the cults, not vice versa. In Galatians, Paul said that anyone who perverts the gospel is accursed. He was not directing the warning specifically to cults, but to anyone. It was a general warning to all that has been applied later to the cults. However, if a group, even though not a "traditional cult," perverts the gospel, the warning and judgment are still applicable.

When Peter, Paul, John, or even Jesus spoke, they spoke of false teachers, not cults. But their warnings are still valid. The church has always had its share of false teachers. Today is no different. The basis for determining a false teacher at that time still applies today.

Why be so concerned about doctrine when experience is what really counts?

There seems to be a growing conflict today between doctrine and experience. However, to elevate experience to the level of scriptural truth can be very similar to the practice of many cults.

Unfortunately, the term "doctrine" evokes feelings of dry and dead lectures, irrelevant discussions, and useless debate. Today, viewing doctrine as bad is a significant danger. Learning doctrine does not have to be like eating Wheaties with no milk. Doctrine is simple biblical truth. Anytime you teach the Scriptures, no matter how simple or how deep, you teach doctrine.

Yet, today there is often a dichotomy drawn between doctrine and experience. Some believe that to be doctrinally well-versed may imply full head and empty heart, especially if your doctrine disagrees with their experiences. It is true that we can *know* in the head but not in the heart. Nevertheless, because we understand doctrine with the head does not mean we cannot have true Christian experience. They are mutually dependent. Every Christian needs both.

It is dangerous to say, "Don't worry about doctrine, just experience God." If our experience does not conform to biblical truth, we may not be experiencing God.

This balance of doctrine and experience has been a problem across many sectors of Christianity. Of great concern to me is the impact today of neo-orthodoxy. We generally call all nonconservative theology liberal. However, many of the tenets of liberalism were found unsatisfying in the early twentieth century, and neo-orthodoxy developed. It is a theology that has one foot on each side of the fence. It retains some of the presuppositions of liberal biblical criticism, but desires a more personal experience with God.

As a result, one of the goals of neo-orthodoxy is to help the individual to *encounter* or experience God. Yet, not recognizing the Scriptures as fully reliable, and feeling that God is generally unknowable, except through personal experience, neo-orthodoxy downplays doctrine. This expresses itself in the phrase, "The Bible 'contains' the word of God, but is not *the* word of God." It is God's word only if God uses it experientially in your life. And of course, God can use any variety of experiences, books, liturgy, etc., to allow you to experience Him.

The result of this is that our experience becomes the most important test of truth, and doctrine less important. We do not use biblical revelation, reason, or apologetics. We must encounter God only through the eyes of "faith," whatever that now means. "God's truth cannot be systematized; that restricts His being." However, if God is truth, and His truth has been revealed in the Bible, then it is logical that His truth would be consistent, harmonious, and systematic. To deny that would be to imply the denial of truthful revelation of God.

Neo-orthodoxy has all the terms and trappings of traditional Christianity, but its emphasis on experience often includes a denial of doctrinal importance and a denial of the Scriptures as a source of reliable, consistent revelation. There are a number of doctrines which are nonnegotiable within the orthodox tradition. Many of these doctrines have been compromised either by non-acceptance or by the greater desire for ecumenical unity.

But doesn't the Bible command us not to judge people?

One person with whom I talked became very antagonistic. "If they believe in Jesus and read the Bible as we do, then they are Christians just like we are, and we have no right to judge them!" I had heard this view expressed many times before, especially in our society, which accepts few absolutes.

Yet, the Bible teaches absolutes. I responded, "Do you believe the Bible is God's written authority for us?" He nodded his agreement. "What if the Bible makes judgments?" I continued.

"Doesn't the Bible teach that there will be false prophets and deceitful workers who will lead people astray?"

"But," he protested, "they believe in the Jesus of the Bible!"

"Who is the Jesus of the Bible?" I queried.

"He's God come in the flesh!"

"What if a group teaches that Jesus is not God come in the flesh? Are they teaching a false Jesus and, therefore, are false prophets?"

"I guess," he conceded.

"Are we being either fair or loving to allow them to be misled? Shouldn't we compare their teachings to the Bible's and make a judgment concerning theirs in order to warn them?"

We must be honest enough to admit that life is based upon making decisions. We must also conclude that one alternative is better than another, that one is right and another is wrong. Since each possible choice will be advocated by someone, we have to make judgments not only about the alternatives but also about the people advocating them.

The Bible honors discernment and good judgment. However, it does not give us the authority to pronounce final condemnation on individuals. God is the final judge. But just because some texts show that God is the final judge of our eternal destinies, we cannot ignore the others which teach that we must make some judgments. Every time we begin to share the gospel, we are assuming that a person is lost. As we share, we are judging whether our assumption is true or false. Should we stop witnessing because it involves some degree of judgment?

Expecting Too Much from a Doctrinal Book

It would be appropriate to conclude this chapter discussing expectations. Often Christians feel that once they are prepared with sound biblical arguments, they will see much fruit when they witness to cultists. This is not generally the case. Evangelism to cults is a field that requires considerable sowing and watering before fruit is seen. Most likely, if the people you share with respond, they will receive Christ much later in a witnessing experience with some other Christian. Very likely, if someone has responded immediately to your gospel presentation, it is because many others have sown seed and watered that seed before you shared with that individual.

There are other important elements in evangelism besides good biblical arguments. A loving attitude and a consistent testimony are essential. Therefore, do not become discouraged if people in cults do not respond to your best arguments when you share with them.

Several years ago, I helped a young man decide to leave a cult. I then discipled him for over three years. After he graduated from the university, he found a job in a town where some members of that little known cult met for worship. It became his ambition to evangelize those people. After his very first contact with them, he and his wife almost reconverted to the cult! Fortunately, I was able to make contact and stabilize them.

They had felt that with their strong biblical arguments, the people would quickly and easily see the light. They were shocked when the cultists had responses to their arguments (as most cultists do). Their responses were not accurate, but they surprised this couple.

Just last year, two Jehovah's Witnesses knocked on our door. Since no one was home at the houses to which they were supposed to visit, they randomly chose our house. They had not consulted with their leaders, because by this time, our house was considered "off limits." As I began to talk with them, they were truly surprised at what the Bible taught and that their organization had revised doctrines over the years. They began asking me many questions. They were eager to learn and were more teachable than almost anyone in my own congregation. After an hour and a half, they finally had to leave. But they insisted on seeing me again.

They never came back. Their authorities quickly began to work with them to keep them within the Kingdom Hall.

One young student at the university where we worked was starting to get involved in a little-known cult. After his sister set up an appointment for us to talk, he saw that the group was unbiblical. However, he felt that there must be answers to my questions, so we met again with one of the cult leaders. He, too, admitted that he could not respond to my questions. He even conceded that if what I was saying was true, then they were following a false prophet, and ultimately, Satan. He was going to bring the highest local leader with him to see me.

The man whom he was bringing was very knowledgeable and had openly challenged the Christian workers and local pastors to a debate. He thought this person could answer my questions. We never met. That summer the group left the university and went to another town. The cult leader who conceded that he might be following a false prophet also went. Fortunately, the young man with whom I first talked left the group. He is in the Christian ministry today.

Yes, there is fruit, a cherished blessing from God. Several years ago, I gave a seminar on the cults from a doctrinal perspective. A lady in the audience taped the lessons because she had a daughter in the Jehovah's Witnesses. When the daughter heard the tape on the identity of Jesus, she broke into tears and responded to the gospel. She did not like what the organization was doing to her marriage. She was fearful, but did not want to leave "the only way to God." When she finally learned what the Bible really teaches, she quickly grasped the truth and was liberated. Jesus said, "You will know the truth, and the truth will set you free" (John 8:32).

While evangelism is comprised of a loving attitude and a consistent testimony, it must also have doctrinal truth. As a matter of fact, if you become involved in evangelizing cultists, you will not be able to escape the doctrinal dialogue. It is the goal of this book to help you develop the doctrinal foundation you need.

PART I

Jesus

More Than a Carpenter: The Identity of Jesus Christ

Wouldn't you have liked to be in my shoes? The audience was 200 eager, and may I say "hungry," philosophy students. My opponent was the chairman of the university's religion department. The moderator, a philosophy professor, had introduced my opponent with a long list of impressive credentials, while I was billed as simply "Bruce Tucker, a staff member of a campus Christian organization." My task was simple: in 45 minutes convince everyone that God exists and then solve little side issues like the problem of evil, omniscience and free will, and something about a mighty God, a huge rock, and a divine hernia. Because of the time limitation, I decided to establish the credentials of Jesus of Nazareth as an honest and respectable authority. On that basis, I could establish His claim that He was God. If He was God, then God clearly exists.

Following my presentation, the religion professor said that the phrase "Son of God" had many meanings, besides being the divine title I said it was. It could mean a descendant of Adam, Abraham, or even King David. It could mean a holy prophet or an angel. Therefore, Jesus' claim to being the "Son of God" meant nothing significant in general, and definitely not deity in particular. Yet, we must admit that Jesus was crucified because of who he claimed to be, and not because of what He did. Thus, it was fairly unlikely that the Jews would crucify Him for being a descendant of Adam, Abraham, or especially King David.

Yet, this entire discussion did present us with an important issue. Who was Jesus of Nazareth? What was meant by the designation "Son of God"? Whenever I attempt to discern if a group is cultic, I always ask first who they say Jesus is. This is a very significant issue in cultic theology.

Interestingly enough, nearly every cult, especially those who rely heavily on the Bible, affirm that Jesus is the Son of God. The Mormons emphatically say, "He is the Son of God, literally, actually. . . ."[1] The Jehovah's Witnesses, who spend considerable time on this issue, refer to Jesus as "the only begotten Son of God."[2]

A growing cult called the Way International holds tenaciously to the biblical designation "Son of God," saying, "In the New Testament Jesus Christ is referred to as God's Son 68 times."[3]

Every major cult (Christian Science, Armstrong's Church of God, and even those Eastern mystical cults) generally consents that Jesus is *a* Son of God. However, this appearance of unanimous recognition is misleading and dissolves rapidly because very few agree as to what the phrase "Son of God" really means.

Shortly after the birth of our twin boys, we were settling into a new house. Our doorbell rang and a nice lady introduced herself as a Christian home missionary who had come to town with a number of others and was canvassing the area. Of course we were excited to meet people involved in home missions doing door-to-door evangelism for Christ. It was not long, however, before I felt the necessity to ask who she felt Jesus was. She responded enthusiastically, "The Bible teaches that He is the Son of God."

I did not feel entirely satisfied with the answer and asked if she could be more specific. She said that of course she could, "Jesus was the Messiah prophesied in the Old Testament who was to come and die for our sins." Again I probed her to be more

---

[1]*What Mormons Think of Christ*, The Church of Jesus Christ of Latter-day Saints (Salt Lake City: Deseret Press), p. 44.
[2]*The Truth Shall Make You Free* (Brooklyn, N.Y.: Watchtower Bible and Tract Society, 1943), p. 49.
[3]Victor Wierwell, *Jesus Is Not God* (New Knoxville, Ohio: American Christian Press, 1981), p. 29.

specific. After using a variety of biblical synonyms such as Messiah, the Christ, the Son of God, Redeemer, we finally discovered that her Jesus was Michael the Archangel, not God come in the flesh. She was a representative of the Jehovah's Witnesses.

Jesus is certainly a unique person. His life is the basis of Christianity. His successful mission on earth was dependent upon His identity. He had to be God to live a life holy enough to be an acceptable sacrifice for sins, yet also a man to fill the role of kinsman redeemer. It is in this tension that the identity of Jesus Christ stands.

He is both God and man, not half God and half man. He is not merely a man overwhelmed with the Spirit of God. He is fully God and fully man. Resolving this relationship of God and man is not easy. We approach it like two-year-olds asking, "How does He do it?" But there is no easy answer. We cannot sacrifice either aspect of His identity. To do so is to turn away from biblical revelation. This is generally the error of the cultist, to deny either Jesus' full deity or His full humanity.

Biblical defenses for either one of these errors are based upon emphasizing one set of scriptures over the other. Accepting both the deity and humanity of Christ is the proper understanding of the phrase "Son of God."

As we mentioned, nearly every cult claims Jesus is the Son of God, and they are quite content when contacting new people to let that phrase stand alone without explanation. But do many cults believe that the phrase "Son of God" includes the aspect of Jesus' deity?

Jehovah's Witnesses define what they mean by "Son of God" in this way:

> So before being born on earth as a man Jesus had been in heaven as a mighty spirit person.[4]

> Being the only begotten Son of God and "the firstborn of every creature," the Word would be a prince among all other creatures. In this office he bore another name in heaven, which name is "Michael."[5]

---

[4]*You Can Live Forever in Paradise on Earth* (Brooklyn, N.Y.: Watchtower Bible and Tract Society, 1982), p. 58.
[5]*The Truth Shall Make You Free* (Brooklyn, N.Y.: Watchtower Bible and Tract Society, 1943), p. 49.

John the Baptist himself was filled with the holy spirit right from his mother's womb. Did John bear witness that Jesus was Jehovah or that Jesus was God? No! John the Baptist told his own disciples: "This one is the Son of God." John said, not "God the Son," but, "the Son of God," an expression meaning something altogether different.[6]

This is further exemplified by the Christian Scientist's definition of "Son of God."

The Christian who believes in the First Commandment is a monotheist. Thus he virtually unites with the Jew's belief in one God, and recognizes that Jesus Christ is not God, as Jesus himself declared, but is the Son of God.[7]

The Son of God to the Way International is not fully God, either.

In other words, I am saying that Jesus Christ is not God, but the Son of God. They are not "co-eternal, without beginning or end, and co-equal."[8]

The Significance of a Wrong Definition

The question persists today, "So what? It does not matter what you believe; it only matters that you believe." But it does matter. Just try driving your car past every gas station *believing* that you won't run out of gas. It is significant because many people can be misled with the same line of reasoning into believing that a specific group is orthodox in their theology while really denying the biblical definition of Jesus.

The Apostle Paul was concerned about taking the historical person of Jesus and changing His true identity.

For if someone comes to you and preaches a Jesus other than the Jesus we preached, or if you receive a different spirit from the one you received, or a different gospel from the one you accepted, you put up with it easily enough. (2 Cor. 11:4)

We find Paul, even in his own time, not only confronting false

---

[6]*The Word—Who Is He According to John* (Brooklyn, N.Y.: Watchtower Bible and Tract Society, 1982), p. 19.
[7]Mary Baker Eddy, *Science and Health with the Key to Scriptures* (Boston, Mass.: The First Church of Christ, Scientist, 1971), p. 361.
[8]Victor Wierwille, ibid., p. 5.

definitions of Christ, but even false Christs (Acts 13:6).

This is important because orthodox Christian faith has always been an objective faith in contrast to a subjective faith. The object of our faith and the credibility of that object are important. We don't want just faith in faith. A vast amount of sincere faith in a rickety old chair will not keep it from collapsing when you sit upon it. Yet a small amount of faith, just enough for you to sit, will uphold you on a very sturdy chair.

Some may feel that since cultists have faith in Christ, they also have a secure faith. But if this were true, Paul would not have been so concerned. To have the authority and blessing of God, you must place your faith in the true Jesus Christ, not a redefined Messiah. More specifically, if you have the wrong Jesus, you will not have the Father either.

> Who is the liar? It is the man who denies that Jesus is the Christ. Such a man is the antichrist—he denies the Father and the Son. No one who denies the Son has the Father; whoever acknowledges the Son has the Father also. (1 John 2:22–23)

John notes that there are many antichrists. They are called antichrists because they deny that Jesus is the Christ (v. 22). He concludes by stating that the Father and Son must be accepted as a pair (v. 23).

John notes in 2 John 9 that one must abide in the teaching of Christ to have God. If one abides in this teaching, one has both the Father and the Son. In his gospel, John makes this even clearer: "He who does not honor the Son does not honor the Father, who sent him" (John 5:23). We do not honor the Son or abide in His teachings of Christ and also deny the full identity of Jesus. This error has significant eternal consequences.

Jesus' Identity in Scripture

The two aspects of Jesus' identity, His deity and His humanity, can be proven by using two texts. In John, Jesus affirms His deity in relationship to the phrase "Son of God."

> For this reason the Jews tried all the harder to kill him; not only was he breaking the Sabbath, but he was even calling God his own Father, making himself equal with God. (John 5:18)

The Jews were seeking to kill Him, not only because He was breaking their traditions, but because He was calling God His Father. John leaves no doubt as to why the Jews wished to kill Jesus, or what he meant by the phrase "Son of God." He was "making himself equal with God."

Nevertheless, Jesus' humanity is explicitly emphasized in 1 Tim. 2:5 in reference to His purpose and mission on earth. "For there is one God and one mediator between God and men, the man Christ Jesus."

Paul is making the case for praying for all the leaders in the world. He does so by stating that God is the only true God in the whole world and that there is only one mediator between God and mankind, the *man*, Christ Jesus.

The term in the Greek found here for "mediator" is usually used in reference to the idea of a kinsman redeemer. The idea of kinsman redeemer is that one from the same family (in this case, the family of mankind) becomes a mediator or restorer. Jesus, to be a true kinsman redeemer, must be from the family of mankind. He must be a true man. Prayer for the world is based upon the fact that one God reigns over the world, that there is only one means of redemption in the world, and that this is through one man, Jesus.

In the following chapters, rather than playing Jesus' deity and humanity against each other, I will attempt to establish both and resolve the tension you have observed between the two.

◆ 3 ◆

The Man Who Stilled the Waters: The Son of God

New Christians are exciting. They are eager to learn about their new faith, they ask honest questions, and they often force the rest of us to think through the basics of our faith in fresh ways.

Our adult Sunday school class was once blessed by an especially inquisitive new believer. One Sunday morning our usually placid class was transformed from the usual 45-minute interlude between coffee and donuts and the morning worship service, to an electric exciting interchange where we all actually learned something.

As I was plodding through a section of one of the gospels, the tranquility was broken by a surprising question. Our new disciple piped up, "If that verse you read says that Jesus is the Son of God, why are you talking as if he was God himself?"

The room was silent, but it couldn't be described as tranquil. For a moment all eyes focused upon this young man; then just as quickly, they were riveted back on me. You could see intense curiosity in the faces of the class members. They wondered, *Well, how is he going to handle this one?*

God has blessed every Sunday school class with an individual who possesses all the answers and "grudgingly" accepts the responsibility of solving issues like these. With definitive tone and authority he responded, "Because He is God."

Fortunately that young Christian had not yet learned to recognize "definitive and authoritative" answers. He came back, "But why was he called the Son of God? He can't be God and God's Son, too, can He?"

Someone else, awakened by the sudden flurry of activity, added, "That is what *Son of God* means, He is God."

"I am confused, then." Puzzled, the young convert continued, "Why didn't the Bible just call him God? Why did it call Him the Son of God?"

This is the question that cultists and Christians wrestle with. Fortunately, the Scriptures give us answers.

Jesus Possesses Divine Attributes

One of the ways that theological thinkers define God is by his attributes. Divine attributes are characteristics distinct to God because only He possesses them perfectly. For example, love is an attribute of God. All men have the capacity to love, but only God is loving in the perfect sense. All men have knowledge, but only God has complete knowledge.

Although many things can be called gods or worshiped as gods, only the God of the Bible has the nature of divinity expressed in His attributes. When Paul wrote his letter to the Galatians, he reminded them that they once served other gods, but that those other gods were not true gods, because they lacked the nature of God (Gal. 4:8).

Jesus Is Omniscient

Jesus possessed the attributes of God. Only God is all-knowing, omniscient. The disciples believed Jesus came from God because He knew all things (John 16:30). John 2:24–25 states that Jesus knew all men as well as what was in man. This is especially significant when placed next to Jer. 17:9–10:

> The heart is deceitful above all things and beyond cure. Who can understand it? I the LORD search the heart and examine the mind, to reward a man according to his conduct, according to what his deeds deserve.

Jesus Is Omnipresent

A second attribute of Deity is omnipresence, God's ability to be everywhere at once. Jesus claims this characteristic in both Matt. 18:20 and 28:20.

Jesus Is Immutable

Because His character is perfect, God never changes. His character cannot be improved upon. This attribute is called *immutability*. "I the Lord do not change" (Mal. 3:6). Heb. 13:8 says that Jesus is the same yesterday, today, and forever.

Jesus Is Eternal

Another characteristic of God is eternality. God has lived forever and will live forever. One of the ways in which the Bible confirms that God is eternal is through the names and titles ascribed to Him.

In Semitic culture, especially in the time of Christ and before, a name described the person. We see examples of this in the New Testament. Simon's name was changed to Peter (meaning "rock"). Jesus' name means "He will save."

God is also given name titles in the Bible. Isaiah uses "the first and the last" to describe God's eternality:

> This is what the Lord says—Israel's King and Redeemer, the Lord Almighty: I am the first and I am the last; apart from me there is no God. (Isa. 44:6)

A similar title describing the same attribute of God, the Alpha and the Omega, is found in Rev. 1:8. Both titles definitely refer to God. That is why it is so significant that Jesus calls himself the "first and the last" and "the Alpha and the Omega."

> When I saw him, I fell at his feet as though dead. Then he placed his right hand on me and said: "Do not be afraid. I am the First and the Last." (Rev. 1:17)

> "I am the Alpha and the Omega, the First and the Last, the Beginning and the End." (Rev. 22:17)

Mic. 5:2 is a prophecy concerning the coming Messiah, who is Jesus. The description of that "coming one" is quite properly rendered in the New American Standard Version as "His goings forth are from long ago, from the days of eternity."

Jesus Is Holy

God is holy. Only He is completely without sin. Nevertheless, Jesus is also described as being without sin in several places (Heb. 4:15; 7:26–27; 1 Pet. 2:22; 1 John 3:5).

> God made him who had no sin to be sin for us, so that in him
> we might become the righteousness of God. (2 Cor. 5:21)

Jesus Is Life

God is life and its author and sustainer. God is also truth. Jesus said, "I am the way and the truth and the life" (John 14:6). Peter in Acts 3:15 states that Jesus was the "author" of life.

The author of Hebrews best summarized the argument that Jesus manifests the attributes of God when he said:

> The Son is the radiance of God's glory and the exact represen-
> tation of his being [nature, NASV], sustaining all things by his
> powerful word. (Heb. 1:3)

However, we must acknowledge some objections to my line of reasoning. Often it is not the attributes of God that are used to prove Jesus' deity but His human attributes that bring His deity into question.

Paul Wierwell of the Way employs this perspective. How could Jesus be considered all-knowing if He did not know every bit of information? The Bible teaches that no one knows the hour of Christ's return, not even the Son (Matt. 24:36). How could Jesus know all things and yet grow in wisdom and stature? (Luke 2:52). How could Jesus be all-powerful if He could not do miracles in His own community because of the people's lack of faith? (Matt. 13:58). How could a baby in a manger be all-powerful? How could a physical human being be everywhere at once?

Remember, Jesus was both God and man, and although the relationship of the human and divine attributes is a mystery, possessing one does not invalidate the existence of the other. If the Bible ascribes divine attributes as well as human attributes, we accept both. We do not ignore one or the other, or promote one at the expense of the other.

Jesus Does What Only God Can Do

Closely related to God's attributes are God's actions. Because of who God is, He has authority to do certain things. Because God is eternal and omnipotent, He alone could be the Creator. If only He has always existed, then everything else which now exists must be the result of His creative power.

In Heb. 1:2–10 we see the creation of the universe attributed to Jesus. Col. 1:15–16 states that He not only created all things, but He also sustains them.

The verses in Colossians say that Jesus is the image of the invisible God, the firstborn of all creation. Of interest in this passage is the term *firstborn*. Jehovah's Witnesses claim it means that Jesus is not God, but God's first creation, an angel, who then created everything else for God.

But "firstborn" need not mean numerical order. The firstborn in Semitic culture is also the one who inherits all the blessings of the father. It is *positional* in emphasis rather than purely numerical. The firstborn is the *highest* rather than just the first.

This is confirmed by a messianic prophecy concerning Jesus in Ps. 89:27. "I will also appoint him my firstborn, the most exalted of the kings of the earth."

Jesus Forgives Sins

Only God is holy. Sin is an affront to Him. He alone has authority to forgive sin (Mark 2:7). The Jews recognized this when Jesus healed the paralytic. They became upset when Jesus said that the paralytic's sins were forgiven. Jesus' response confirms His authority.

> "Which is easier: to say to the paralytic, 'Your sins are forgiven,' or to say, 'Get up, take your mat and walk'? But that you may know that the Son of Man has authority on earth to forgive sins. . . ." He said to the paralytic, "I tell you, get up, take your mat and go home." (Mark 2:9–11)

Jesus Receives Worship

God alone, because of His nature, is deserving of worship. When people attempted to worship the apostles, the apostles stopped them (Acts 14:14–15). In the Book of Revelation, the Apostle John attempted to worship the angel who gave the revelation, and the angel refused the worship (Rev. 22:9).

Nevertheless, Jesus is worthy of worship. The author of Hebrews proclaims, "Let all God's angels worship him" (Heb. 1:6). Even more significant is the fact that Jesus did not rebuke the Apostle Thomas when he worshiped Him, nor when he called Jesus his Lord and God (John 20:28).

Titles of God Are Ascribed to Jesus

As we were mentioning the eternality of Jesus, we appealed to the use of the title, the "first and the last." There are other titles of deity which are applied to Jesus Christ. The term "Lord" (*Kurios*), can mean either God or a term of respect, such as "sir." But in Rom. 10:9 the term is applied to Jesus when it clearly means God.

> That if you confess with your mouth, "Jesus is Lord," and believe in your heart that God raised him from the dead, you will be saved.

In John 1, John the Baptist identifies himself for the priests by using a prophecy from Isaiah:

> "I am the voice of one calling in the desert,
> 'Make straight the way for the Lord.' " (John 1:23)

The prophecy in Isa. 40:3 speaks of the Lord (*Kurios* in the Greek version) as Jehovah God. A messenger would come to prepare the way for Him. John identifies himself as this messenger and then, later in John 1, speaks of Jesus as the object of his preaching. We must accept the fact that he is identifying Jesus as Jehovah God by calling Him "Lord," just as Isaiah had.

Jesus Is the Holy One

Who does the name "the Holy One" refer to in the Bible? Isa. 48:17 makes it clear that God is "the Holy One." Yet, Peter, when preaching his Pentecost sermon, called Jesus "the Holy and Righteous One" (Acts 3:14).

Jesus Is the Savior

Like the new believers in Samaria in John 4:42, we all acknowledge that Jesus is the Savior of the world. But how often do we recall Isa. 43:11, "I, even I, am the Lord, and apart from me there is no savior"?

The angel told Joseph that they should name him "Jesus" because He would save His people from their sins (Matt. 1:21). In the same context it says, "And they will call him Immanuel"— which means, "God with us" (Matt. 1:23).

Important Testimony

As in any legal case, evidence must be presented and testimony evaluated. If I told you that I was God, you would not believe me without evidence, would you? In the New Testament, a number of authors noted the testimony of the early followers of Jesus, their own perceptions, and the words of Jesus himself. Who did they think Jesus was? Better yet, who did Jesus say He was?

When evaluating the testimony of the New Testament authors, I will devote the most space to a few important texts and then respond to arguments to those texts by two cults, the Jehovah's Witnesses and the Way International.

The Testimony of Jesus

One of the most significant texts identifying Jesus as God is found in John 8. Jesus was in a discussion with the Pharisees. As the discussion grew more intense, the Pharisees detected that Jesus was claiming supremacy not only over the prophets but even Abraham. Upon hearing this, they demanded that Jesus clarify himself by stating directly who He was (v. 53). As the dialogue evolved, Jesus responded so specifically that He ended the conversation. Jesus said to them, "Before Abraham was born, I am" (John 8:58).

The Jews immediately understood Jesus' intent and reached for stones with which to kill Him for blasphemy. As we look closer at the passage, we can see why the Jews responded in such a fashion.

The important element in the text is the contrast between Jesus' existence and Abraham's existence. Jesus is saying much more than that He existed before Abraham. He declares the quality of that existence. The clause "I am" (*ego eimi*) is in present tense. In the Greek language, this describes a continuous action. It means "one who continues to exist." (The Appendix has a technical explanation of the grammar used here.) The Greek says that Abraham "came into being" or "was born." The point is clear, before Abraham was "born" or "came into being," Jesus continually existed.

If John had wanted to say that Jesus simply existed before Abraham, he would have implied that Jesus was born or came into existence just as Abraham, but only at an earlier date.

The Jehovah's Witnesses have spent considerable time in altering this verse. Their first attempt was to classify the verb "am" (*eimi*) as a "perfect indefinite tense" rather than the present tense.[1] But there is no such thing as a "perfect indefinite tense" in the Greek.

They also try to say that the phrase is better translated "before Abraham, I was." They will do some Greek gymnastics trying to prove this.

Their answer sounds good, but means very little. Jehovah's Witnesses commonly attempt to intimidate people with a Greek "snow job." Much of what they say concerning the Greek is wrong, and most is irrelevant.

As I share these insights with Christians, they respond that the Jehovah's Witnesses do intimidate them with the Greek, and they ask how to discuss the issues on that level. My advice to them is that unless you understand the use of the Greek in a specific case, do not discuss it! I have encountered many Jehovah's Witnesses who were eager to discuss the Greek with me until they discovered that I was familiar with the language; then I never heard the Greek referred to again. Most of them do not understand any more Greek than you. They are probably just as intimidated as you.

Therefore, if they try their Greek on you, find out how much Greek they have studied and then agree to stick to the English that you both understand. Suggest a Bible translation that would be acceptable to both of you. Several cults have their own translations with most of their favorite "errors" corrected, but most will also agree to use the King James Version.

As we boil all the elements of John 8:58 or any other passage down, we should be left with the same understanding that the Jews had: Jesus was claiming deity.

---

[1]Walter Martin, *Kingdom of the Cults* (Minneapolis, Minn.: Bethany House Publishers, 1985), p. 87.

The Testimony of the Author of Hebrews

The author of Hebrews in the first chapter of his epistle demonstrates the superior revelation of God in His Son. The revelation through His Son is superior to all other revelation because of its nature and quality. It is personal, not just verbal or literary, and its revealor, Jesus, is greater than any other revelation because He is God's Son.

What is the Son like, and who is He? He is heir of all things (v. 2). He is the maker of the world (v. 2). He is the radiance of God's glory. He upholds all things by the word of His power. And after making purification of sins, He sat down at the position of authority in heaven (v. 3). These descriptions define attributes of deity, which is not surprising, because the author prefaces these statements by saying that the Son is the exact representation of God's nature. Divine nature and attributes can be possessed to this extent only by God.

Jesus Is Higher Than the Angels

Next, the author compares Jesus to the angels, and the Son is found to be superior. Rhetorically the author asks a question to prove the superiority of the Son, "For which of the angels did God ever say, 'You are my Son, today I have become your Father'?" (v. 5). The answer is clear from the style of the question that there is no angel.

Nevertheless, Jehovah's Witnesses contend that the question seeks to evoke one answer: Michael. Yet, this is not a plausible response, because the author answers the question by describing the function of all angels. The angels are just ministers (v. 7), and they are all commanded to worship Him, the Son (v. 6), an action reserved only for God!

However, the most significant evidence for the identity of the Son is found in verse 8 where the Father, addressing the Son, calls Him God.

> But about the Son he says, "Your throne, O God, will last for ever and ever, and righteousness will be the scepter of your kingdom." (Heb. 1:8)

God the Father certainly understands the identity of the Son and will not lie. When He calls the Son "God," it carries a significant amount of weight.

Though the verse is straightforward, the cultist is likely to fight the translation on anything which states Jesus' divinity so strongly. Since these are technical grammatical arguments, we have given them to you in the Appendix.

The Testimony of the Apostle Paul

Paul is responsible for a significant number of the New Testament epistles and several references dealing with the deity of Christ.

Of particular interest is Titus 2:13: "While we wait for the blessed hope—the glorious appearing of our great God and Savior, Jesus Christ." The key issue in this passage is whether or not the term "God" modifies Jesus Christ. If so, Paul believes that Jesus is God. In that case we are expecting the return of one person, Jesus, who is described as our great God and Savior.

On the other hand, Jehovah's Witnesses contend that we are expecting the return of the great God, Jehovah, and our Savior, Jesus Christ. Where one places the comma becomes important. Fortunately, we can confidently assert that one person, not two, is referred to. Jesus is both our Savior and our great God.

The reason is that this construction falls under the authority of an interpretive rule called the Granville Sharp rule. (You will find it in the Appendix.)

Peter also gives testimony of Jesus' deity and employs the same usage in 2 Pet. 1:1:

> Simon Peter, a servant and apostle of Jesus Christ, to those who through the righteousness of our God and Savior Jesus Christ have received a faith as precious as ours.

The Testimony of the Apostle John

Of all the authors of the New Testament, John most clearly attempts to identify Jesus Christ. He concludes his Gospel:

> But these are written that you may believe that Jesus is the Christ, the Son of God, and that by believing you may have life in his name! (John 20:31)

In the beginning of his gospel, John says:

In the beginning was the Word, and the Word was with God, and the Word was God. (John 1:1)

Further in this chapter John becomes more specific:

The Word became flesh and lived for a while among us. We have seen his glory, the glory of the one and only Son, who came from the Father, full of grace and truth. (John 1:14)

The clearest conclusion is that the Word was God, and that this Word became a man. The text refers to Jesus, the Son of God. This is a very important verse establishing the deity of Christ.

The Jehovah's Witnesses claim that the best translation of verse one is not "the Word was God," but "the Word was a God." They base this on the fact that the Greek has no "the" (*ho*) before "God"; therefore the translation is "the Word was a God."

We have already mentioned the credentials the Jehovah's Witnesses have for translating Greek. Needless to say, their interpretation of the verse is based more on fear of the true meaning than on Greek grammar. The verse actually leaves little to be questioned as we know it in our English versions. Technical arguments for this are available in the Appendix at the end of the book.

When the Apostle John said that Jesus was God, he was accurately understanding what Jesus claimed for himself and what the Jews understood Him to say.

"I and the Father are one." Again the Jews picked up stones to stone him, but Jesus said to them, "I have shown you many great miracles from the Father. For which of these do you stone me?" "We are not stoning you for any of these," replied the Jews, "but for blasphemy, because you, a mere man, claim to be God." (John 10:30–33)

John records the statement by the Jews here as sure proof of what Jesus meant when He spoke of His deity. Jesus could have corrected a wrong impression here and calmed the angry mob, but He continued undeniably stating that He was God.

Your Testimony

Now that we recognize the fullest meaning of the phrase "Son of God," how do we use this information in evangelism? The first and best answer is to use the Scriptures I have given with discretion. I, as an author, have had to be more comprehensive in establishing the deity of Christ. When you are talking with a cultist, do not back the dump truck up to them and unload everything you have. Pick a few strong arguments for Jesus' deity and then use the rest of the information to respond to further questions. Do not feel obligated to use all the evidence.

Second, be alert to how the cultist toys with the phrase "the Son of God." I once sat with another pastor who told me how he loved describing Jesus as the Son of God because it kept the old ladies off his back. He told me he thought that Jesus was *a* divine son of God, as we all are, and an example of what we could all be if we just put our mind to it. He knew his congregation would balk if he told them directly what he believed, but he took shelter in the phrase's ambiguity to give him time to mold his congregation into accepting his definition. With time he was successful.

Sometimes a person can discern what someone believes about Jesus' identity from what he does not say more than by what he does say. For instance, one of our relatives was asking us how to find a good church in their part of the country. This is a question with which we have all wrestled. There is no simple answer to this question, but a crucial ingredient is finding what a church believes about the identity of Christ. If someone dodges a direct answer to Jesus' identity, and dwells in ambiguity, then you should ask more specific questions. Do not settle for the single answer that He is the Son of God.

◆ 4 ◆

The God in Swaddling Clothes: The Son of Man

Jesus once sent His disciples out to witness and to serve people. When they came back, they were overjoyed at the power they had found in the name of Jesus.

I once sent some disciples out too. They were going to visit a friend who did not believe in the deity of Christ. Armed with a few "decisive verses," some arguments from Josh McDowell, and a bit of prayer, they went off to convince an individual of the truth.

When they returned, they appeared less like conquerors in Christ and more like little puppies with their tails between their legs. "Bruce," they said, "he had answers to our arguments." Feeling betrayed by me, God, and Josh McDowell, and fairly humbled, they had not come to realize that there are responses, but not necessarily answers.

Out it poured, "If Jesus is equal to the Father, why did He say that the Father is greater than I? Why did He pray to the Father, and thus submit himself to Him? Why were there things He did not know? If God is Spirit, why did Jesus have a body?" Less confident, more humbled, less easily satisfied with quick answers, they began to study these issues again.

The most significant problem individuals have in accepting the deity of Christ are the passages that bear witness to the fact that Jesus is also a very real man. The deity passages play against the humanity passages and vice versa. That causes tension. We cannot exclude one set of texts; both are true. The problem is in seeing how both can be true!

Some use this difficulty to contend that the Bible is contradictory. Some from a more liberal background use this conflict as a basis for dating the Gospel of John very late, saying that the concept of the deity of Christ as John presents it evolved with time, because of the overenthusiastic worship of exaggerating believers. Some attempt to bring both sets together by compromising one truth or the other, making Jesus more divine or more human. Nevertheless, Jesus was fully God, and also fully man.

Jesus Possessed Human Attributes

All of us, being human, recognize what human attributes are. We have bodies of flesh and bones. We get tired; even college students do! We need lots of sleep and lots of food. We grow older, then die.

Jesus had all of these characteristics too. He was born (Luke 2:8–20). He became hungry (Matt. 4:2) and thirsty (John 19:28). He became tired (John 4:6), and He slept (Matt. 8:24). He also died (John 19:30). He experienced the emotions that men feel. He felt compassion (Matt. 9:36), and He wept (John 11:35). He was troubled, distressed, grieved, and suffered (John 12:27; Mark 3:5; Heb. 2:10, 18).

In reference to our nature, mankind is said to be comprised of two parts, the material and the immaterial. Jesus was an individual who possessed our flesh (John 1:14) and a rational mind or soul (*psuche*) (John 12:27). Jesus possessed human attributes.

Jesus Possessed Human Titles and Offices

Just as titles describe Jesus as being God, human titles are also attributed to Jesus. Jesus had a family tree and was called the son of a number of human ancestors, such as the son of Joseph, Mary, David, and Abraham.

Jesus was a prophet (Luke 24:19), a priest (Heb. 5:6–10), and a king (Luke 1:31–33), all of which are human offices.

Testimonies of Jesus' Humanity

Paul called Jesus a man in a number of places (Rom. 5:15; 1 Cor. 15:21; 1 Tim. 2:5).

The Apostle Peter agreed with Paul. In his first sermon on the day of Pentecost he preached that the man Jesus was put to death. If the group of disciples could be classified as a church board, then we have at least one deacon's meeting where there was consensus: they all claimed Jesus was a man. "The men were amazed and asked, 'What kind of man is this? Even the winds and the waves obey him!' " (Matt. 8:27).

It is very interesting that in the same conversation where Jesus called himself God (John 8:58), He had earlier called himself a man. "As it is, you are determined to kill me, a man who has told you the truth that I heard from God. Abraham did not do such things" (John 8:40).

Human and Divine

As confusing as it may be, and as confused as you may be right now, the fact is that Jesus is one person who possesses two natures, divine and human. Unfortunately, how this is possible is not fully explained. But, the truth is clear in the Scriptures. Our willingness to accept this fact depends upon our submission to the Bible.

The divine and human interplay in the person of Christ pervades the New Testament. For example, we read in Acts 20:28:

> Guard yourselves and all the flock of which the Holy Spirit has made you overseers. Be shepherds of the church of God, which he bought with his own blood.

In this verse, Paul is charging the elders of the Ephesian Church to care for the flock, to shepherd the church of God, which He purchased with His own blood. It is a church of *God*, which *He* purchased with His physical human blood.

Paul, when writing to the Corinthians, said that the Lord of glory was crucified (1 Cor. 2:8).

Divine characteristics are also linked with human titles. In Rom. 9:5, Jesus is referred to as a descendant of Israel. At the same moment, He is given the divine characteristic of being "over all."

Similarly, preexistence is a trait of God. John combines the trait of preexistence with a human title, the Son of Man. "What if you see the Son of Man ascend to where he was before!" (John 6:62).

The angel said that the human child Jesus was to be called Immanuel—God with us (Matt. 1:23).

The Son of Man

Even though all Christians are children of God (John 1:12), Jesus is the only begotten Son of God. This title emphasizes His deity. The purpose of Hebrews, chapter one, is to teach that Jesus is the Son of God, and, therefore, divine. Consequently, it is very interesting that the second chapter of Hebrews discusses Jesus as the Son of Man, emphasizing the concept of His humanity.

On the basis of several rhetorical questions in Hebrews, chapter one, we learned that Jesus has inherited a better name than all of the angels. Now, in the second chapter it states that Jesus was made a little lower than the angels.

> It is not to angels that he has subjected the world to come, about which we are speaking. But there is a place where someone has testified: "What is man that you are mindful of him, the son of man that you care for him? You made him a little lower than the angels; you crowned him with glory and honor and put everything under his feet." In putting everything under him, God left nothing that is not subject to him. Yet at present we do not see everything subject to him. But we see Jesus, who was made a little lower than the angels, now crowned with glory and honor because he suffered death, so that by the grace of God he might taste death for everyone. (Heb. 2:5–9)

The emphasis of "Son of Man" is His humanity and His purpose for being a man. Through His ministry as a man, He would bring many sons to glory (v. 10), who are His brothers (v. 11). His death, which was only possible if He was human, destroyed the power of the devil (v. 14) and delivered mankind from spiritual slavery (v. 15). To be a faithful high priest (a human intercessory office) and a propitiation for sins (a sacrifice requiring a body), He had to be human.

> For this reason he had to be made like his brothers in every way, in order that he might become a merciful and faithful high priest in service to God, and that he might make atonement for the

sins of the people. Because he himself suffered when he was tempted, he is able to help those who are being tempted. (Heb. 2:17–18)

Jesus was the Son of Man. All humans are also called the sons of man because we are of the human race. But just as the phrase "Son of God" was unique to Jesus, so is the phrase "Son of Man." "Son of Man" also has messianic implications.

The prophet Daniel discussed this unique Son of Man:

> In my vision at night I looked, and there before me was one like a son of man, coming with the clouds of heaven. He approached the Ancient of Days and was led into his presence. He was given authority, glory and sovereign power; all peoples, nations and men of every language worshiped him. His dominion is an everlasting dominion that will not pass away, and his kingdom is one that will never be destroyed. (Dan. 7:13–14)

The uniqueness of the title is substantiated by the response it provokes at the trial of Jesus. When Jesus claimed to be the Son of Man and equated himself with the one in the prophecy of Daniel, the high priest condemned Jesus for blasphemy (Mark 14:61–64). Of special interest is Luke's description of the trial. In this context it is not only clear that the title "Son of Man" is important, but it even equates the meaning with the title "Son of God" and "Christ."

> "If you are the Christ," they said, "tell us." Jesus answered, "If I tell you, you will not believe me, and if I asked you, you would not answer. But from now on, the Son of Man will be seated at the right hand of the mighty God." They all asked, "Are you then the Son of God?" He replied, "You are right in saying I am." (Luke 22:67–70)

Both titles carry the same divine significance, but they emphasize different aspects of Jesus' nature.

The Purpose and Mission of the Incarnation

What we have been discussing and has been so difficult to comprehend is that the God of the universe stepped out of the heavenly dimension and became a human being. This is the doctrine of the incarnation: God took on human flesh and bones and dwelt among us.

Why? We have alluded to this answer several times before, but now let's be more specific. First of all, He became incarnate to manifest and reveal the incomprehensible God. As John said, "No man has ever seen God" (John 1:18). But the Son has manifested Him. Paul says in Col. 1:15 that Jesus is the image of the invisible God. God is invisible, but the only begotten Son reflects Him.

When you watch a film on a movie screen, you see an image. The light and colors projected from the projector are not fully visible or understandable until they make contact with a physical screen. In a similar way, Jesus is both the light from the projector, the invisible God, *and* the screen. He is both, not just one or the other. He is not a normal man merely overpowered with God, nor just a man with more divine consciousness than most. He is one person who is both divine and human. As the author of Hebrews (1:3) states: "The Son is the radiance of God's glory and the exact representation of his being."

Is God evil? Can we trust Him? As people discuss philosophically, they attempt to get a picture of God and His nature from discussions of His attributes and how He acts in history. What kind of God would wipe out the tribe of the Philistines, including women and children? How could He be loving and still advocate war? In many of the Old Testament stories, we see a mixed picture of a merciful God and a God of wrath.

Some have contended, from a more liberal stance, that man developed the concept of God. As mankind became more sophisticated, they created God in their own image. Since man was prone to war in Old Testament times, mankind defined God as a warrior. By the time Jesus appeared on the scene, mankind believed in peace, so Jesus defined God in a new way.

So, what is God like? Philosophically, is He that evil being who does not eliminate the problem of evil? How accurately can we reconstruct a picture of God when we look at a word puzzle with 95 percent of the pieces missing?

But Jesus is the exact representation of God's nature. We see the life, attitudes, and actions of Jesus in historical context. We see His love, mercy, and also His wrath! Do we ever indict Jesus as the evil God philosophers sometimes picture? Never. Jesus reveals God in a complete context without all the missing pieces.

Besides revealing the invisible God, Jesus had a mission: to seek and to save the lost (Luke 19:10). Only God is holy enough to redeem mankind, but only a man could be a kinsman redeemer and a sacrifice for His brethren. The passages we read in which the apostles emphasized the humanity of Christ were in the context of Jesus' work as redeemer and sacrifice.

Paul's words to Timothy are a clear example. "For there is one God and one mediator between God and men, the man Christ Jesus" (1 Tim. 2:5). The context is Paul's command to pray on behalf of all men, including kings and men in authority. Why does Paul say that this is proper? Because God desires all of mankind to be saved and come to a knowledge of the truth. Why does Paul feel that all mankind can be saved? Because in all the world there is only one God—the God of the whole world, and only one mediator—a mediator for the whole world, Jesus the man. Why the emphasis on the term man? Because He is a ransom for all (1 Tim. 2:6).

The idea of a ransom is rich in cultural meaning. It was used for the buying back of slaves, the paying of a debt, or the avenging of a crime by a family member. This is where we get the concept of a *kinsman redeemer*.

A kinsman redeemer was an individual from the family who either avenged the death of another family member, or paid the debt for a family member. Redemption also carried the aspect of sacrifice in Jewish history. It is clear in this context that Jesus was not only the sacrifice for sins, but also the kinsman redeemer, one of the family of man who paid the price for His brethren. Consequently, His humanity is emphasized. When the Scriptures speak of Jesus' work of salvation, they speak of Him as a man. Paul teaches that Jesus is the firstfruits. He is the second Adam who corrects the fall of the first Adam. He is the first man to be resurrected and never die again.

> But Christ has indeed been raised from the dead, the firstfruits of those who have fallen asleep. For since death came through a man, the resurrection of the dead comes also through a man. For as in Adam all die, so in Christ all will be made alive. But each in his own turn: Christ, the firstfruits; then, when he comes, those who belong to him. (1 Cor. 15:20–23)

Job quite properly understood the need for a unique mediator between God and man when he said, "For He is not a man
as I am that I may answer Him, that we may go to court together.
There is no umpire between us, who may lay his hand upon us
both" (Job 9:32–33, NASB). The word for "umpire" in the Greek
version of the Old Testament is also found in 1 Tim. 2:5 for
"mediator."

Therefore, Jesus fulfilled His mission of redeeming mankind
as an actual man. True, He was a special man, conceived by the
Holy Spirit, but a man, nevertheless.

The Kenosis

The idea of God becoming a man and the intricacies of that
relationship is the kind of idea in which it is difficult to tie all the
loose ends together. It sounds like a plausible solution, but the
question persists, "Is there any text which teaches clearly that
Jesus existed before as God, became a human being, and then
ascended back into heaven?" Fortunately, there is.

Philippians, chapter two, is considered the classical *kenosis*
passage that describes this truth. *Kenosis* is the Greek term meaning "emptying." It describes what took place when God became
a man.

> Your attitude should be the same as that of Christ Jesus: Who,
> being in very nature God, did not consider equality with God
> something to be grasped, but made himself nothing, taking the
> very nature of a servant, being made in human likeness. And
> being found in appearance as a man, he humbled himself and
> became obedient to death—even death on a cross! Therefore
> God exalted him to the highest place and gave him the name
> that is above every name, that at the name of Jesus every knee
> should bow, in heaven and on earth and under the earth, and
> every tongue confess that Jesus Christ is Lord, to the glory of
> God the Father. (Phil. 2:5–11)

The context of this section is an exhortation to the Philippian
Christians to be more humble. To drive that point home, Paul
uses Jesus as an example of humility. Jesus existed in the very
nature of God before He was born to Mary.

Since Jesus existed in the form of God, He was the expression of the nature of the Divine. But now being found in human "likeness" (*schema*), meaning the outward, changeable appearance, He did not regard equality a thing "to be grasped" (*arpagmon egesato*), an idiom that means "to exploit for one's own advantage." Instead, He humbled himself in the form of a bondservant and was made in the likeness of a man. The result was that after His death on the cross, Jesus was highly exalted.

Jesus himself discussed this principle with His disciples in John 17.

> After Jesus said this, he looked toward heaven and prayed: "Father, the time has come. Glorify your Son, that your Son may glorify you. For you granted him authority over all people that he might give eternal life to all those you have given him. Now this is eternal life: that they may know you, the only true God, and Jesus Christ, whom you have sent. I have brought you glory on earth by completing the work you gave me to do. And now, Father, glorify me in your presence with the glory I had with you before the world began. (John 17:1–5)

Because Jesus was functioning in the role of a man, He could not glorify himself. But notice in this passage that He commands the Father to glorify Him. This is especially clear in verse 5 where the command verb form is used. But what kind of glory does He wish? The same glory which He had before the world was! He had glory before the world was, and it was a shared glory with the Father.

From all eternity, the eternal Son shared glory with the eternal Father. After His incarnation, while fulfilling His function as a man, He set aside His glory. But now He commands that the shared, equivalent glory which He had with the Father before now be restored.

Why did Jesus humble himself so much? Paul gives the answer in 2 Cor. 8:9: "For you know the grace of our Lord Jesus Christ, that though he was rich, yet for your sakes he became poor, so that you through his poverty might become rich."

Conclusion

The identity of Jesus is a very important issue to understand and to communicate. It can give direction and strength to your evangelism, and keep you from getting sidetracked. For example, a high school student in my church recently asked me about a specific problem text in the Book of Proverbs. In a discussion with some Jehovah's Witnesses, he was finding himself constantly involved with a number of obscure texts about a variety of different issues.

It is common for the cultist to use such a "shotgun approach." A vast number of topics are initiated so that the Christian becomes overwhelmed with the responsibility of answering a constant barrage of questions.

It is not the responsibility of the Christian to disprove all the doctrines of any cult. Good theology is not developed in a court of law, where the doctrines advocated by a cult are assumed true until the church disproves them. It is the responsibility of the cultist to prove their doctrines biblically, not of the church to refute every speculation that is advanced.

I could assert that the planet Mars has intelligent life and then demand that Christians biblically prove me wrong. But just because they may discover it impossible to find relevant biblical texts that disprove my assertion beyond the shadow of a doubt does not make my assertion true!

Moreover, even if the cultist finds obscure Bible verses that appear to justify his unique doctrines, it does not mean that you have to answer them. Many issues are simply smoke screens. Answering them will accomplish little except to take away time from crucial issues and weaken your confidence.

This is why the identity of Jesus Christ is such an important issue. It does not matter if I believe there is life on Mars. If I have the wrong definition of Jesus Christ, I am wrong on the most important issue. It is this issue, the identity of Christ, which has significant implications on eternal life.

I recommended to the young man in my church that he restrict his discussion to this issue, and urge the Jehovah's Witnesses with whom he was talking, to do the same. If they refused to limit themselves to this issue, then it would be very unlikely that he would be able to change their minds. In dialogues with most cultists, this will be the most important issue. A strong background in this area will go a long way in evangelizing the cults.

Study Questions For Part I

1. Who is Jesus Christ?
2. What does "Son of God" mean?
3. Can a group which states that Jesus is the Son of God be a cult?
4. How serious is it to have the wrong definition of Jesus?
5. Is Jesus God?
6. How do we know that He is God?
7. Which attributes does Jesus possess that suggest His divinity?
8. What abilities does Jesus possess that suggest His divinity?
9. Which titles ascribed to Jesus suggest His divinity?
10. Which biblical texts testify to Jesus' divinity?
11. What does "Son of Man" mean?
12. Is Jesus a man?
13. Which attributes, actions, and titles suggest that He is a man?
14. Which texts testify to Jesus' humanity?
15. How can Jesus' deity and humanity be explained?
16. Why must Jesus be God to redeem mankind?
17. Why must Jesus be a man to redeem mankind?
18. Which texts testify to this unique relationship?
19. How do the cults deviate from these truths?
20. How do the cults attempt to justify their deviations?
21. Why are the cults incorrect in their interpretations?

Part II

The Trinity

The Trinity

• 5 •

Explaining the Three-in-One in Human Language

My wife and I sat across the living room from another young couple who had been involved in the Jehovah's Witnesses for just a few months. They had visited us before and found some of our questions difficult to answer. As a result, they were back a second time. This time they brought a man with them who they were confident could answer all our questions. We put our dog in the backyard, their kids in the front yard, turned off the TV, and unplugged the phone. There was only one intruder in the way of a good discussion: an appeal to the improper use of reason.

Every cult, when confronting the doctrine of the Trinity, will often appeal to reason as the foundation for discussion. This is natural because the Trinity may well be one of the most difficult concepts for the Christian to understand.

Consequently, that morning when our guest began by quoting "Come now, let us reason together" (Isa. 1:18), there was no doubt that before long, I would appear to be very unreasonable. No one wishes to be "unreasonable," least of all me, and no one tends to be persuaded by "unreasonable" people, most of all me. Yet providentially or not, I filled the role of the unreasonable person that day.

Almost every cult denies the orthodox definition of the Trinity. Most pastors avoid teaching on the Trinity because it is so complex, and many Christians simply do not understand it.

The Definition of the Trinity

Although the term "Trinity" is not found in the Bible, neither are many other terms which the church has coined to identify a concept that Scripture presents. For example, one does not find "missions" in the Scriptures, yet few in the church deny that Christ commanded us to be involved in missions. Many hold the term "rapture" very dearly. Yet, that term is not found in the Bible either. The same is true of "Trinity."

What is the Trinity? Let me provide a working definition:

> While God is one, he is comprised of three equal, coexistent, coeternal, yet distinct persons, the Father, the Son, and the Holy Spirit, who each function in different roles.

There are four crucial elements in the definition of the Trinity:

1. The oneness of God.
2. The plurality of three persons.
3. The equality of the three persons.
4. The distinction and simultaneous existence of the three persons.

The Trinity is not *tri-theism*, three separate Gods. It is not one person with different titles. Three distinct persons are referred to in the Scriptures. These three are all considered to be God, and yet God is one. Finding a home for all these facts without violating some of the truth is the source of the doctrine of the Trinity. Deviations from the doctrine of the Trinity develop from attempting to find harmony with all the facts, but with the result of denying some of the crucial elements.

Confusion from Human Limitations

If you have paused to adequately think about the Trinity, then you will be able to admit how confusing it can be. It's something like a third grader trying to understand quantum physics. I can easily understand why people can be confused about the concept, especially those who must have all their ideas neatly boxed in proper categories, all their *t*'s crossed and *i*'s dotted.

People often become frustrated because they are not satisfied with limited answers to difficult questions. Therefore, from the very beginning it would be good to recognize that there are limits to what we will be able to understand and why these limits exist. We must also be willing to submit in faith to what God's Word says concerning this doctrine. If we are discussing the nature of God, certainly His input is not only important, but necessary for accuracy.

The Limitation of Human Reason

As human beings, we are fairly proud of our ability to reason. Nevertheless, if God is infinite and we are finite, then our ability to understand Him is limited. Our minds are gifts from God that separate us from the animals, but they also set us apart from God, whose reason and knowledge is incomprehensible.

The debate is not new as to how reliable reason is. Thomas Aquinas was convinced that reason remained perfect and unaffected by the fall of man. Therefore, man could logically deduce God. By contrast, the reformers held strongly to total depravity, all aspects of man were affected by the Fall, reason included. In the realm of spiritual issues, 1 Cor. 2:14 seems to say that certainly reason itself is inadequate. This is the basis for Paul's contention that wisdom will not lead man to God.

> Where is the wise man? Where is the scholar? Where is the philosopher of this age? Has not God made foolish the wisdom of the world? For since in the wisdom of God the world through its wisdom did not know him, God was pleased through the foolishness of what was preached to save those who believe. (1 Cor. 1:20–21)

However, let us remember that reason is good. I reason with my children just as my wife does with me. Christianity is reasonable. The ultimate theological marriage is reason plus revelation. But when revelation, clearly and properly interpreted, conflicts with reason, then reason must submit itself to God's revelation. Thankfully, this is the exception in theology, not the rule.

Look at figure A on the next page. The circle represents mankind's scope of understanding. It is finite and limited in comparison with the universe and God's omniscience. The lines represent ideas and concepts that exist within the universe. Some concepts pass through our circle of understanding, but many do not. We remain totally ignorant of their existence.

Some lines intersect within our scope of understanding and we can comprehend how those ideas relate (note Fig. B). For example, we understand the effects of gravity and we understand solid objects. If we were to drop a bowling ball from a twelve-story building, we would have a fairly concrete idea of what will happen.

However, some issues enter our circle of understanding but do not intersect there. As a result, we are unable to reconcile and understand them. These issues cause us concern. For example, a benevolent God and present evil, predestination and free will, or one God comprised of three equal persons all confuse us because they seem to be paradoxes.

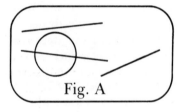

Fig. A

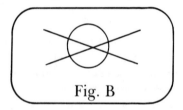

Fig. B

We should be careful not to make these issues a source of too much concern, because if we really feel that mankind is finite, we should expect paradoxes. It would be consistent with what we know about man and God.

The conclusions of this illustration are important. Just because two concepts do not intersect within our circle of understanding does not mean that they cannot intersect outside our circle of understanding (note Fig. C on next page). If we really believe that we are limited in our knowledge, then we would expect that some concepts that we are not able to reconcile could intersect outside our circle of understanding. What would not be correct is to say that if we cannot understand how two concepts can intersect, then one cannot be true.

If God, then, reveals that two concepts are true, even if we do not understand them, we must accept them by faith (note Fig. D). Not willing to accept our limitations, we often force two concepts to intersect within our circle of understanding and thus compromise or violate the original truth.

Of course we could resolve this problem if we could expand our circle of understanding infinitely. But only God is omniscient.

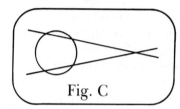

Fig. C

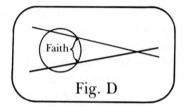

Faith

Fig. D

Just because we are unable to reasonably answer a question does not deny the existence of that truth. Historically the Trinity doctrine has never been based upon reason but upon divine revelation. What God says has been the basis of truth, not what we can neatly package. God has never been obligated to reveal more than He chooses, and neither can we know more about Him than He chooses to reveal.

The Limitation of Human Language

God has chosen to reveal His truth through human language and human language is adequate to reveal that which God has chosen. However, human language may not be adequate to explain some issues we find irreconcilable.

Language development is based upon analogies. Our vocabulary depends upon concrete experience and previously learned vocabulary. Analogies build upon one another to give us a more specific and complex vocabulary. A child understands the term "ball" because he can see one. He understands the term "soft," a more abstract concept, because he has touched a satin blanket and a fuzzy teddy bear.

The fewer the analogies and illustrations of a concept, the greater the chance for confusion. This relates to the concept of the Trinity, because there is no accurate analogy in our world for the Trinity. Consequently, it is difficult to comprehend.

Whenever I make that statement, I receive an immediate and ardent protest from everyone. The average layman to the most influential pastor all insist upon the fact that their particular illustration provides an accurate analogy. However, although there may abound illustrations of three parts and oneness, none can be applied fully as a complete illustration of the Trinity without violating some of the crucial elements of the definition of the Trinity. Yes, they can be helpful in demonstrating the idea of multiple parts being one. However, the problem is that the Trinity encompasses more than that idea alone, and expanding these analogies can be counterproductive.

For example, it is often said that the Trinity is like a man who, although being one, is simultaneously a son, a father, and a husband. He may also be a brother, an uncle, a grandfather, a godfather, or a neighbor. This common illustration simply demonstrates a major cultic error, modalism, which says that God is one person, not three, with a variety of titles.

Some insist that God is like a family of three persons. Herbert W. Armstrong holds this view and thus changes the meaning of oneness.

Other illustrations have major problems too. It is true that an egg is comprised of three parts, but does the yoke have the same nature as the shell? A triangle has three sides, but is any one side fully a triangle, or just a third of a triangle? Is Jesus a third of God, or is He fully God?

I think one of the best illustrations is that of water. Under controlled conditions (at a constant pressure and at exactly 32°F.), it can be a vapor, a solid, and a liquid all at once. These illustrations can help ease our confusions, but they are not adequate analogies. When we note their limitations, the paradox still exists. The lack of an exact analogy does cause confusions.

The complexity of the nature of God also causes confusion.

We understand new concepts and terms as we are able to assimilate them into the grid of our previous experience. This conceptual understanding grows and becomes more specific as we are able to make previous knowledge more concrete. The more concrete the concept, the more we are able to understand it.

With words, the more abstact the term, the more difficult the definition. We all experience love, but philosophers, poets, and teenagers can define it only by using descriptions from their previous experiences, each defining "love" with vastly divergent meanings. In other words, the more concrete the terms and the more experiential analogies, the easier the concept is to understand. The more abstract the concept and the fewer the analogies, the more confused our understanding.

Defining an infinite God becomes extremely difficult because all efforts to define His nature must be based upon our finite experiences and analogies. In Scripture, the Holy Spirit has used *anthropomorphic terms*, human analogies to describe the infinite God. These analogies offer some descriptions, but they still fall short. God is called a Father. He has arms long enough to save, eyes that can see in the dark, and He never sleeps. Being a spirit, God does not need sleep. It is difficult to teach the concept that God always is aware of us and our actions. Unfortunately, it leads some to believe that spirits have physical characteristics. Besides using anthropomorphisms, the Holy Spirit uses the many names of God in an attempt to describe the nature of God.

It is always difficult to describe infinite concepts in finite terms to finite people. When does time begin? How far does space extend? We say, "Forever." But none of us desires to dwell on these infinite concepts too long. We have no concrete analogies with which to understand them and it makes us feel uncomfortable and inadequate. God is infinite and we have no good analogy for His existence.

After I had a short discussion one evening with a college freshman, he said he could not believe in God because he could not understand God. He said if I could clearly explain how God could be infinite, he would believe. I asked if he could first tell me how far space extends. He said that was impossible to answer. I asked him when time began and what it was. He said there was no answer. I responded by saying these were concepts of an infinite nature that he encountered and discussed frequently in his own finite world. Because he could not clearly define them did not nullify their existence; it simply demonstrated how frustrated we can become when we encounter issues outside our circle of understanding.

A finite level of language certainly becomes a barrier to the physicist explaining quantum mechanics to a first grader. With the child's limited vocabulary and conceptual experiences to draw upon, he may hear the scientist say that his skateboard is comprised of moving particles with space between them. But he will, more than likely and in very elementary terms, communicate that there is an irreconcilable contradiction in a solid pine board having moving electrons. This does not mean that the skateboard is not solid, or that quantum mechanics is false. It simply demonstrates that limited vocabulary and limited conceptual experience will likely cause confusion and misunderstanding in very complex issues.

The effects of this complexity can also be seen in defining glass. When you tap your knuckles on wood, steel, or concrete, you conclude that they are solid. And when you tap your knuckles on a window, you would logically conclude that it, too, is a solid. Your conceptual experiences say that objects that feel hard and "clunk" when tapped are solid. However, any chemist will tell you that glass is not a solid, but a liquid!

Generally, our experiences can provide definitions that are true. However, some issues require more than a general understanding; they require special, more in-depth analysis. Glass is one. The molecular movement may be slow, but according to my chemistry teacher, it is a liquid.

The same is true of some theological issues. On a general level they seem reasonably clear, but on a more detailed level, the accurate definition may be beyond our grasp, even seemingly contradictory.

The Trinity is a very abstract and complex concept. Therefore, it can cause confusion. But just because of the complexity and just because there are no complete analogies does not mean that the Trinity cannot be true!

Revelation, the Basis of the Doctrine of the Trinity

If there are limitations to our finite understanding of infinite issues, and if language, although adequate to communicate what God chooses, is limited, then how can we know about God? The answer is found in the fact that God chose to reveal himself to man in the Scriptures. Once we recognize our limitations, we can accept what God's revelation teaches, no more and no less. Revelation then becomes the foundation not only for what we believe but also how we live. Because Scripture is God's Word, it will be confirmed in those areas where it is demonstrable. In those areas outside our ability to verify, like the definition of the Trinity, we accept them by faith, knowing that if God wanted us to know more clearly, He would have been more specific. It is His choice, not ours. If there are gaps in this information, it is because God chose to leave these gaps.

The Trinity Is a Mystery

These gaps are called biblical mysteries. Cultists find this view unacceptable. What is a theological mystery? Is a doctrine defined as a mystery automatically false? Can there be biblical doctrines that are mysteries and still be true? Because the doctrine of the Trinity is a mystery, it does not necessarily follow that the Trinity doctrine is false.

A biblical mystery can be defined as a concept which is beyond our scope of understanding, but which could be understood if God chose to give more revelation. There are a number of mysteries in the Bible. For example, in Rom. 16:25–26, Paul talks about the gospel of Jesus Christ being preached as the revelation of the mystery which was kept a secret, but is made manifest. Earlier, in Rom. 11:25, Paul explains the meaning of a mystery by giving more revelation. He does this because he does not want the Romans to remain in ignorance.

In Matt. 13:11 Jesus explains why He has been speaking in parables; so that those He wants to understand the mysteries will be able to understand, and those He does not want to understand will remain blinded. Clearly, more revelation could explain a biblical mystery. Why should Jesus watch His words so carefully? Many mysteries have been explained in the Bible, some have not. The Trinity has been revealed but not clearly explained. It is a biblical mystery. Nevertheless, it does not follow that it must, therefore, be false.

Tensions with Revelation as a Basis

Revelation is the foundation for determining truth. Many would agree with this, but often we find three competitors to revelation: feelings, experience, and reason. When revelation disagrees with our feelings, we will often discount revelation. When revelation contends with our experience or circumstances, we will often give credence to our experience. This is especially true in mystical cults and even with many Christians who emphasize experience. Finally, when revelation and reason line up on the opposite sides of the fence, sometimes we find the grass greener on the side of reason.

Unfortunately, this places reason above Scripture as a greater authority. This assumes that a finite individual is more knowledgeable or trustworthy on the subject of God's nature than God himself.

A second tension with revelation is *selective biblicity* or *prooftexting*. Limiting the texts which are relevant to a specific doctrine may help create a neat theological package, but it may also be false. Good systematic theology demands that all the relevant passages be taken into consideration. This may make the issue much more complex, but it will also eliminate simple and inaccurate solutions. Many deviations to the doctrine of the Trinity are the result of selective biblicity.

•6•

Defending the Trinity

The basis for the doctrine of the Trinity is the Bible, the revelation of God. As a matter of fact, if we had no Bible, there would be no doctrine of the Trinity. Man, of his own initiative and insight, could never deduce the Trinity. This is consistent with our finiteness and God's incomprehensibility.

However, I have encountered very creative people who exemplify the *need* for authoritative revelation like the Bible. Once I talked with a college student about the deity of Christ. He claimed that Christianity was mythology. He claimed there was no rational evidence for the deity of Christ. After going through the evidence for the resurrection, it seemed clear to me that Jesus' claim to be God was confirmed in his resurrection.

At that point, the student leaned back, rubbed his chin, and suggested that Jesus was an ancient astronaut. I was curious. Why, then, did Jesus claim to be God? He responded, "Since He was an ancient astronaut in a primitive culture that believed in gods, claiming this would protect His life." Unfortunately, this astronaut was not up on his social anthropology, because the Jews crucified Him for His claim.

Undaunted, the young man answered, "Astronauts are able to rise from the dead!" Instead of answering my question, it only produced another. Then why did Jesus, a wise ancient astronaut, claim to be God to preserve His own life if He had the ability to resurrect all along?

If we are our own authority, we may be creative, but also inconsistent and incorrect. Fortunately, the Bible does give us reliable information. On that basis we will establish the elements of the doctrine of the Trinity.

God Is One

Christianity as well as Judaism is monotheistic. Jews believe in only one God. Deut. 6:4 is the classic Old Testament text cited to establish this position. "Hear, O Israel: The Lord is our God, the Lord is one!"

There are no other gods but Yahweh. The New Testament also affirms that there is one God. "So then, about eating food sacrificed to idols: We know that an idol is nothing at all in the world and that there is no God but one" (1 Cor. 8:4). Other passages also testify to this fact: 1 Kings 8:60; Deut. 4:35; 1 Tim. 2:5.

God speaking through the prophet Isaiah affirmed His own nature when He said:

> "I am the first and I am the last; apart from me there is no God." (Isa. 44:6)

> "You are my witnesses. Is there any God besides me? No, there is no other Rock; I know not one." (Isa. 44:8)

> "I am the Lord, and there is no other; apart from me there is no God." (Isa. 45:5)

Jesus himself when questioned by the scribes on the greatest commandment, testified to the oneness of God.

> "The most important one," answered Jesus, "is this: 'Hear, O Israel, the Lord our God, the Lord is one.' " (Mark 12:29)

There is no lack of biblical evidence that there is only one God.

The Plurality of God

In the Old Testament, the mystery of the plurality of the Godhead was introduced, even though not fully explained. In the creation account, the author of Genesis used plural pronouns in reference to God:

> Then God said, "Let us make man in our image, in our likeness, and let them rule over the fish of the sea and the birds of the air, over the livestock, over all the earth, and over all the creatures that move along the ground." (Gen. 1:26)

Do the plural pronouns refer to angels? No. "Let *us*" and "in *our* image" refer directly back to God and no one else. We know this because they are pronominal elements which are attached to the verb itself. This is common in Hebrew. Elohim is speaking and He says, "let *us* make." "Us" refers back to Elohim.

Some have attempted to find the plurality of the Godhead in the term "Elohim." However, even though the term is plural, it is a Semitic plural of majesty, emphasizing the magnitude of God by using the plural form. But it is not a reference to plural persons in and of itself. Elohim is not only a Hebrew term, but also a general term for God used by other peoples of that time. Nevertheless, in the first book of the Old Testament, God used plural pronouns to refer to himself.

Similarly, plural pronouns in Ps. 2:1–3 help us to recognize the plurality of God.

> The kings of the earth take their stand and the rulers gather together against the Lord and against his Anointed One. "Let us break their chains," they say, "and throw off their fetters." (Ps. 2:2)

The Messiah is the Son of God (v. 7). We have already established that Jesus, the Son of God, is fully God. This text refers to the Lord *and His* Messiah (Anointed One). Why does the author make a distinction between two persons, the Lord and His anointed, who is also God?

Previously, we quoted Deut. 6:4, which stated that God is one. We may now go a step further in reference to the plurality of God. The Hebrew term for "one" (*echad*) carries the idea of composite unity. It is a term for "one" that allows for diversity. On the other hand, if the idea of absolute unity were to be expressed, another term (*yachid*) would have been used.

The Person of the Father

In our Western theological culture, we have always assumed that God is personal. The title "Father" is personal. However, many cults are now based upon an Eastern world view, *monism*, which does not necessarily agree that God is personal. Who is right? Is the Father really a person?

He has personal attributes that we would hesitate to apply to a nonhuman force. For example, as we simply pray the Lord's prayer from Matt. 6:6–15, we recognize that we are conversing with the Father. From this passage alone we can list a number of personal attributes. He rewards, sees, hears, knows, forgives, leads, delivers, and has a personal will. Once you accept the Scriptures as God's revelation, there are innumerable references to His personality.

Similarly, it is not difficult to demonstrate that the Father is also God. The introduction to many epistles uses the construction, "God the Father" or "God our Father" (Rom. 1:7; 1 Cor. 1:3; 2 Cor. 1:2; Gal. 1:1; Eph. 1:2; Phil. 1:2; Col. 1:2; 1 Thess. 1:1; 2 Thess. 1:1). The fact that He is distinct from the Son is clear in 2 Pet. 1:17–18.

> For he received honor and glory from God the Father when the voice came to him from the Majestic Glory, saying, "This is my Son, whom I love; with him I am well pleased." (2 Pet. 1:17)

There are several passages which show an interaction between the Father and the Son as separate persons. We will look at some later in this chapter.

The Person of the Son

In Part One of this book, I took considerable time developing the fact that Jesus was fully God. It was also clear by the fact of His incarnation that He was a person.

Jesus, as the Son, was certainly personal and distinct from the Father. As we discussed the plurality of God, we saw someone called the Anointed One in Psalm 2. Later in that chapter God calls Him His Son. Prov. 30:3–4 also presents a distinction between the Son and the Father. The passage refers to the Holy One and lists some of the acts of God. It concludes by saying, "What is his name, and the name of his Son?"

The Person of the Holy Spirit

Probably the most difficult person of the Trinity to establish is the Holy Spirit. This is due to a variety of reasons. For example, since His role is one of a servant in the Trinity, coming to glorify

Christ (John 16:14), we find that teaching about His identity is less direct than with Jesus, whose divinity was important to recognize. However, the texts we do have are clear.

A very common mistake concerning the Holy Spirit is to identify him simply as *God's active force* and not a person. Yet, Scripture is quite clear as to His personality and His deity. One of the reasons the Spirit is considered only an active force by cultists is that the term for Spirit (*pneuma*) in the Greek is a neuter word. Since many appeal to the Greek to deny the Holy Spirit's deity, we will need to delve into the Greek to respond.

All nouns in Greek are one of three genders: masculine, feminine, or neuter. Greek nouns take different endings depending upon how they are used in a sentence. But even when the endings change, the nouns must still keep their distinctive gender.

But just because a term is grammatically masculine does not mean it is masculine in gender. Wenham's grammar demonstrates this principle.

> In Greek, gender has to do with the form of the words and has little to do with sex. There are masculine, feminine and neuter forms, but "bread" is masculine, "head" is feminine, and "child" is neuter.[1]

Some ethereal things like love, truth, and peace are closest to being neuter, so are called *abstract nouns* in Greek, but are all feminine in gender. "Spirit" (*pneuma*) is categorized as neuter probably because it is based upon the word for wind (*pneua*), which is neuter. You see, we must be careful how we evaluate genders or Greek nouns.

When "Spirit" or (*pneuma*) is used in the New Testament, it keeps its neuter ending. Words that modify it must also use the neuter ending. Therefore, it is very significant that when the Apostle John speaks of "this Spirit" in John 16:13–14, he uses the masculine pronoun.

> "But when he [*ekeinos*—masculine], the Spirit of truth, comes, he will guide you into all truth. He will not speak on his own [*heautou*—masculine or neuter]; he will speak only what he hears, and he will tell you what is yet to come. He [*ekeinos*—

---

[1] J.W. Wenham, *The Elements of New Testament Greek* (Cambridge: Cambridge University Press, 1979), p. 8.

masculine] will bring glory to me."

Because gender is grammatical and not sexual in most nouns, pronouns usually distinguish male people, female people, and neuter things. Thus, John is ascribing male personality to the Spirit.

In Eph. 1:13–14, Paul does the same thing John has done. He speaks of "the promised Holy Spirit, who (*ho*—masculine) is a deposit guaranteeing our inheritance . . ."

In John 15:26, we see the combination of two terms for the Holy Spirit, "spirit" and "comforter" (*pneuma* and *paracleitos*). "Spirit" is neuter, but "comforter" is masculine.

> "When the Counselor (*paracleitos*—masculine) comes, whom I will send to you from the Father, the Spirit (*pneuma*—neuter) of truth who goes out from the Father, he will testify about me."

This verse introduces the term "counselor" (*paraclete*), a masculine term for the Holy Spirit. This is important for several reasons. First, it demonstrates that while "spirit" (*pneuma*) is neuter, the Holy Spirit is also referred to by a masculine term. Of course, the implications of this are limited because of what we have already said about the meaning of gender in Greek. Nevertheless, one can no longer contend that no masculine words identify the Holy Spirit.

Second, *paracleitos* is the term used in Classical Greek for an advocate or lawyer. This usage is personal, not abstract.

Third, *Paraclete* is also used of Jesus Christ in 1 John 2:1. Jesus can hardly be considered an abstract idea. Jesus prayed in John 14:16 that the Father would send another comforter, the Spirit of Truth. "Another" (*allon*) implies a comforter of the same kind, like himself, a personal advocate.

The Jehovah's Witnesses do not identify the Holy Spirit as a person, but as *God's active force*. In their text *You Can Live Forever in Paradise on Earth*, they base part of their claim on the analogies of water baptism.

> As for the "Holy Spirit," the so-called third Person of the Trinity, we have already seen that this is not a person but God's active force. John the Baptizer said that Jesus would baptize with holy spirit, even as John had been baptizing with water. Hence, in

the same way that water is not a person, holy spirit is not a person.[2]

But as we study the references in relation to the Holy Spirit's activities, we see that He is described as having the personal attributes of intellect, emotion, and will. He does what a person does. He convicts (John 16:8), teaches (John 14:26; Neh. 9:20), speaks (Gal. 4:6; Acts 10:19), intercedes (Rom. 8:26), leads (Acts 8:29; 13:2), and appoints (Acts 20:28).

The Holy Spirit is affected as a person is affected. He can be sent (John 14:16, 26; 16:7), quenched (1 Thess. 5:19), blasphemed (Matt. 12:31), grieved (Eph. 4:30; Isa. 63:10), lied to (Acts 5:3), disrespected (Heb. 10:29), and spoken against (Matt. 12:32).

It may be true that the Scriptures use some nonpersonal analogies like water to describe the Holy Spirit, but to explain them all as personifications would be difficult. It is hard to lie to a fire, disrespect the wind or to grieve any inanimate force.

Moreoever, not only is the Holy Spirit a person, but He is also God. Peter tells Ananias in Acts 5:3, 4 that the man has lied to the Holy Spirit. At the end of his accusation, Peter says that the lie was made to God. He presents the words as interchangeable, and thus equates God and the Holy Spirit.

Just as the Holy Spirit has the attributes of a person, He also possesses attributes of deity. Divine attributes can be possessed only by God. He is omniscient (1 Cor. 2:9–11; Isa. 40:13–14), omnipresent (Ps. 139:7–10), omnipotent (Luke 1:35), the giver of life (Job 33:4), eternal (Heb. 9:14), creator (Gen. 1:2), not to mention the fact that He is obviously a *holy* Spirit.

Finally, the Holy Spirit is also identified with God as the giver of revelation. For example, two quotations credited to God in the Old Testament are attributed to the Holy Spirit in the New Testament.

---

[2]*You Can Live Forever in Paradise on Earth* (New York: Watchtower Bible and Tract Society, 1982), p. 40.

Isaiah
Then I heard the voice of the Lord saying, "Whom shall I send? And who will go for us?" . . . He said, "Go and tell this people: 'Be ever hearing, but never understanding; be ever seeing, but never perceiving.' " (Isa. 6:8–9)

Acts
"The Holy Spirit spoke the truth to your forefathers when he said through Isaiah the prophet: 'Go to this people and say, "You will be ever hearing but never understanding; you will be ever seeing but never perceiving." ' " (Acts 28:25–26)

Jeremiah
"This is the covenant I will make with the house of Israel after that time," declares the Lord. "I will put my law in their minds and write it on their hearts. I will be their God, and they will be my people." (Jer. 31:33)

Hebrews
The Holy Spirit also testifies to us about this. First he says: "This is the covenant I will make with them after that time, says the Lord. I will put my laws in their hearts, and I will write them on their minds." (Heb. 10:15)

The Distinctiveness of the Persons

Three divine persons are mentioned in the Scriptures. The Scriptures also teach that God is one. In an attempt to harmonize these facts, some, especially groups called "Jesus Only" churches, insist upon the solution that all three are simply one person. This is reasonable, but incorrect.

The Scriptures teach clearly that these three persons are distinct from each other and also coexistent. They exist at the same time, not during different periods of history. Coexistence is simply a logical conclusion. If all three are God, then all three must be eternal because eternality is an attribute of God.

As we mentioned earlier, in Genesis, chapter one, we find plural pronouns attached to the verbs that refer to God. The only conclusion must be that somehow God is both one but also a plurality. Because there was little additional revelation at that time, the mystery was unclear. Additional revelation has helped resolve part of the mystery.

There are several biblical texts that refer to all three persons of the Trinity. Jesus himself provides the classic text:

"Therefore go and make disciples of all nations, baptizing them in the name of the Father and of the Son and of the Holy Spirit, and teaching them to obey everything I have commanded you. And surely I will be with you always, to the very end of the age." (Matt. 2:19–20)

The author of the epistle to the Hebrews also mentioned all three persons as he discussed Christ's sacrifice on the cross.

> How much more, then, will the blood of Christ, who through the eternal Spirit offered himself unblemished to God, cleanse our consciences from acts that lead to death, so that we may serve the living God! (Heb 9:14)

When Peter was once speaking to the Gentiles, he also acknowledged three persons.

> How God anointed Jesus of Nazareth with the Holy Spirit and power, and how he went around doing good and healing all who were under the power of the devil, because God was with him. (Acts 10:38)

Even in the Old Testament, where the doctrine of the Trinity had not been fully developed, there is a reference to the three persons. In Isaiah, chapter 48, God identifies himself as the one who called Israel (v. 12). He calls himself the "First and the Last" (v. 12). He is the one who founded the earth (v. 13).

At this point God begins to speak of His elect one, the Messiah, Jesus. Then the servant speaks. He is not just the prophet, because we see references to His preexistence. In verse sixteen, we see the chosen one being sent with the Spirit by the Lord.

Besides the references that simply mention the three persons, several texts show an interaction between the persons. For example, at the baptism of Jesus we read:

> As soon as Jesus was baptized, he went up out of the water. At that moment heaven was opened, and he saw the Spirit of God descending like a dove and lighting on him. And a voice from heaven said, "This is my Son, whom I love; with him I am well pleased." (Matt. 3:16–17)

Some people have falsely declared that "the Father" was the facet or title of God revealed in the Old Testament, "Jesus" was the title of God while He was incarnate, and the Holy Spirit is the way God presents himself after the resurrection.

One form of this view has its roots in an early heresy called "adoptionism," which believed that God came over the man Jesus and "adopted" His body to hold Deity. Adoptionists would contend that this passage simply demonstrates that moment of transition. Adoptionism is generally not the view of the "Jesus Only" groups today, because adoptionists do not advocate a unity of the person of Christ. However, they do hold to the shifting emphasis of different facets of the Godhead.

But even so, after the baptism of Jesus, we see further interaction between the persons. At the transfiguration of Jesus, God the Father identifies the Son and speaks to Him.

> While he was still speaking, a bright cloud enveloped them, and a voice from the cloud said, "This is my Son, whom I love; with him I am well pleased. Listen to him!" (Matt. 17:5)

Similarly, there is another experience where the Father speaks from heaven.

> "Father, glorify your name!" Then a voice came from heaven, "I have glorified it, and will glorify it again." The crowd that was there and heard it said it had thundered; others said an angel had spoken to him. (John 12:28–29)

Unless Jesus was a ventriloquist, or found a purpose in misleading His followers, it was the Father, another distinct person of the Trinity, talking with Him.

Conclusion

The Bible teaches that God is one and that three persons are that one God. It also teaches that they have eternally coexisted. Confusing? Yes. But to eliminate one of those revealed truths in an attempt to relieve theological tension is to deny revealed truth and to enter into the domain of cultic theology.

Distorting the Trinity

More than any other doctrine, the doctrine of the Trinity is a clear measure of cultic theology. Many cults can confuse the new proselyte about the person of Christ, even ardently claiming His deity. Cults often insist on salvation by grace through faith even though more thorough research confirms that the definitions of some crucial words and concepts have been altered. However, once an individual clearly understands the Trinity, distortions of this doctrine are difficult to disguise. Therefore, many cults are proud of being non-Trinitarian and have no desire to cloud their strange view of the Trinity. Consequently, this doctrinal deviation is one of the most identifiable and prevalent.

A sure red light when discussing theology is the denial of the orthodox doctrine of the Trinity. Most Christians are confused about it and therefore insecure about discussing it. The Trinity is difficult to understand and requires faith as well as submission to revelation. Yet, to call God something other than who He is is inappropriate. Be aware of these common errors:

1. Changing the one God to three or more Gods. (3 persons = 3 Gods)
2. Changing the three persons to just one person. (1 God = 1 person)
3. Changing the three persons to three manifestations or titles of one person.
4. Changing the meaning of "person" to an abstract impersonal force or idea.

Deviations from Oneness

As we have already seen, God is one. The demons even acknowledge this fact and tremble because of it (James 2:19). However, since Paul says that some abandon the faith because of the influence and teaching of demons (1 Tim. 4:1), we might assume there are deceitful spirits who wish to deny the oneness of the God they fear.

Historically this error is called *polytheism*, the belief in many gods. The basis of this view is the overemphasis on the three persons of the Godhead. If there are three persons, the argument goes, then the persons must be separate gods.

The Mormons are an example of this view. Although claiming to be Trinitarian, they see the heavens filled with a pantheon of other gods. In this scheme, the Father is one god, Jesus another, and Lucifer, another spirit being, is another god. *The Pearl of Great Price*, a Mormon scripture, describes the creation as the work of many gods.

> And then the Lord said: "Let us go down. And they went down at the beginning, and they, that is the Gods, organized and formed the heavens and the earth."[1]

In a commentary on *The Doctrine and Covenants*, in reference to Sec. 76:23, the meaning of "the Son of God" is described as the only begotten of the Father.

> God the Eternal Father, whom we designate by the exalted name title Elohim, is the literal parent of our Lord and Savior Jesus Christ, and of the Spirits of the human race. *** Jesus Christ is the Son of Elohim, both as spiritual and bodily offspring; that is to say, Elohim is literally the Father of the Spirit of Jesus Christ, and also of the body in which Jesus Christ performed His mission in the flesh. . . .[2]

Nevertheless, Mormons claim to follow only one God. What they hold to is the concept of *henotheism*, not *monotheism*. Both terms are derived from the Greek words for "one," but with different meanings. Monotheism believes that there is only one God. Henotheism believes that, while there are many gods, we should only worship one of them. Mormons believe not only in the existence of a hierarchy of gods, but even that God the Father has gods above Him. One respected Mormon elder said:

---

[1]Abraham 4:1, *The Pearl of Great Price*.
[2]Hyrum M. Smith and Janne M. Sjodahl, *Doctrine and Covenants Commentary* (Salt Lake City, Utah: Deseret Book Co., 1950), p. 448.

"Mormonism" claims that all nature, both on earth and in heaven, operates on a plan of advancement; that the very Eternal Father is a progressive being; that his perfection, while so complete as to be incomprehensible by man, possesses this essential quality of true perfection—the capacity of eternal increase. That therefore, in the far future, beyond the horizon of eternities perchance, man may attain the status of God. Yet this does not mean that he shall be then the equal of the Deity we worship, nor that he shall ever overtake those intelligences that are already beyond him in advancement; for to assert such would be to argue that there is no progression beyond a certain stage of attainment, and that advancement is a characteristic of low organization and inferior purpose alone. We believe that there was more than the sounding of brass or the tinkling of wordy cymbals in the fervent admonition of the Christ to his followers: "Be ye therefore perfect, even as your Father which is in heaven is perfect."[3]

As you noted in the quotation, Mormons have the potential to become gods.

Herbert W. Armstrong and the Worldwide Church of God is another group that alters the Trinity doctrine. Armstrong denies that the Holy Spirit is the third person of the Trinity. He also believes that "before Jesus was conceived by Mary, He was not the Son of God. . . . He is called the *Logos*—the Word."[4]

Armstrong believes in a "God family," not a Trinity:

The Eternal Father is a Person, and is God. Jesus Christ is a different Person and is God. They are two separate and individual Persons (Rev. 4:2; 5:1; 6–7). The Father is the Supreme Head of the God Family. . . . And the wonderful truth is that human beings may be born into this same ONE God Family as distinct, separate Personalities by a resurrection from the dead.[5]

But does he really mean that we become divine persons?

All who NOW are begotten sons of God shall then be BORN-elevated from mortal to IMMORTAL, from decaying FLESH to SPIRIT—from HUMAN to DIVINE![6]

---

[3]James Talmage, *The Articles of Faith* (Salt Lake City, Utah: Deseret Press, 1970), p. 530. (Quoted from James Talmage, *The Story and Philosophy of "Mormonism,"* pp. 108–110.)

[4]Herbert W. Armstrong, "Just What Do You Mean: Born Again?", *The Plain Truth*, February 1977, p. 34.

[5]Herbert W. Armstrong, "Is Jesus God?", *The Plain Truth*, June 1977, p. 38.

[6]Herbert W. Armstrong, "Just What Do You Mean: Born Again?", ibid., p. 35.

What is the basis for this deviation? Certainly these people must use the Bible as a basis of their faith! Often cited to establish this perspective is 1 Cor. 8:5.

> For even if there are so-called gods, whether in heaven or on earth (as indeed there are many "gods" and many "lords").

The Bible teaches that Satan is the god of this world (2 Cor. 4:4). There are many things that we make or call gods, but they are not God by divine nature. "Formerly, when you did not know God, you were slaves to those who by nature are not gods" (Gal. 4:8).

The Lord himself, speaking through the prophet Isaiah, made it quite clear that there were no other gods and that there would be no new ones.

> This is what the Lord says—Israel's King and Redeemer, the Lord Almighty: I am the first and I am the last; apart from me there is no God. Who then is like me? Let him proclaim it. Let him declare and lay out before me what has happened since I established my ancient people, and what is yet to come—yes, let him foretell what will come. Do not tremble, do not be afraid. Did I not proclaim this and foretell it long ago? You are my witnesses. Is there any God besides me? No, there is no other Rock; I know not one." (Isa. 44:6–8)

Interestingly enough, the idea that we can become like God has a biblical origin.

> "You will not surely die," the serpent said to the woman. "For God knows that when you eat of it your eyes will be opened, and you will be like God, knowing good and evil." (Gen. 3:4–5)

Deviating from the Plurality of the Godhead

The second way that the Trinity is distorted is overemphasizing the oneness of God. Since God is one, then He must be only one person. Any other persons mentioned must not be fully God.

This is a denial of the equality of Jesus and the Holy Spirit with the Father. It has roots in an early heresy espoused by a man named Arius and his followers, Arians. The classic modern example of this deviation is the Jehovah's Witnesses. They emphasize the oneness of Jehovah but deny that Jesus and the Holy

Spirit are God. Jesus to them is a created being, Michael the Archangel, and the Holy Spirit is simply "God's active force."

The Way International also deviates from the doctrine of the Trinity in this way. To them, Jesus is not God, but first existed when born of Mary in Bethlehem. Before this time he existed only in the mind and foreknowledge of God the Father.

> Where was Jesus Christ before he was born to Mary? Jesus Christ was with God in His foreknowledge.[7]

Unitarians, as indicated by their name, are also not Trinitarian.

> In general, a Unitarian is a religious person whose ethic derives primarily from that of Jesus, who believed in One God—not the Trinity. . . . Unitarians hold that the orthodox Christian world has forsaken the real, human Jesus of the gospels, and has substituted a "Christ" of dogmatism, metaphysics and pagan philosophy. Because Unitarians refuse to acknowledge Jesus as their "Lord and God," they are excluded from the National Council of Churches of Christ.[8]

> Unitarians repudiate the doctrine and dogma of the Virgin Birth. . . . Unitarians do not believe that Jesus is the Messiah either of Jewish hope or of Christian fantasy. They do not believe he is "God incarnate" or "the Second Person in the Trinity" or the final arbitrator at the end of time who "shall come to judge the quick and the dead."[9]

The Firstborn

There are several errors that allow this incorrect perspective to flourish. The first is the error of the firstborn. This error refers to an incorrect interpretation of Col. 1:15, "He is the image of the invisible God, the firstborn over all creation."

The Jehovah's Witnesses insist that "firstborn" in this context speaks of birth order, that Jesus had a beginning and that His beginning was the first beginning of all creation. However, the context speaks of Christ being the creator of all things. "For by him all things were created" (Col. 1:16). He cannot have created

---

[7]Victor Wierwille, *Jesus Is Not God* (New Knoxville, Ohio: American Christian Press, 1981), p. 30.

[8]Carl M. Chorowsky, *Look Magazine*, "What Is a Unitarian?", March 8, 1955, p. 77.

[9]Chorowsky, ibid., p. 78.

himself. He stands separate from creation.

The meaning of "firstborn" here is "positional preeminence." He has been appointed "firstborn" by the Father just as David was firstborn among the kings of the earth (Ps. 89:27). Jesus is the high and exalted one over all creation.

Victor Paul Wierwille of the Way has a different problem with this text. If, according to Wierwille, Jesus first existed at His physical birth, then He could not have been the firstborn of creation, either numerically or positionally. He contends that verse 15 refers to God the Father, while all the rest of the verses refer to the Son. He claims that the verse is a figure of speech called a *parenthesis*, where another idea is inserted into the text for explanation. However, all the verses begin with pronouns which all have one common antecedent, the Son. Wierwille's contention is grammatically impossible.

Compared Roles

A second error is the error of compared roles. As the members of the Trinity function in their different roles, missions, responsibilities, they subordinate themselves to each other. But the Jehovah's Witnesses and other cults will point to the inequality of the roles and state that Jesus cannot be God because He is not as great. The text usually cited is John 14:28:

> "You heard me say, 'I am going away and I am coming back to you.' If you loved me, you would be glad that I am going to the Father, for the Father is greater than I."

As Jesus speaks, He is fulfilling His function as a priest. He will die on the cross, ascend to heaven where He will intercede for His brethren. This passage defines a number of roles. For example, verse 26 says that the Father will *send* the Holy Spirit. In verse 31, Jesus speaks of His *obedience* to the Father. His subordinate role to the Father does not make Him less than the Father. It merely illustrates a role Jesus had accepted in the plan to redeem mankind. Quite accurately within the context of roles, the Father is greater, but not necessarily better.

In a human example, the Scriptures teach that men and women are equal (Gal. 3:28). But the man is head over the woman (1 Cor. 11:3). They are equal, but with different roles.

Authority

A third error would be the error of delegated authority. John 17:2 is often noted as a basis for this error. "For you granted him authority over all people that he might give eternal life to all those you have given him."

This error is similar to the preceding one. If Jesus was functioning in a subordinate role and was also fully man, then He as a man would also have had to place himself under the authority of the Father. While functioning in this way, He would have to have been given authority from the Father to have any at all.

As you can see, these three errors arise from the fact that Jesus was fully man, and from the implications of that very unique relationship. As we explained in Part One, the tension between His deity and humanity cannot be resolved in the denial of part of the revealed truth. The Bible clearly teaches that Jesus was fully God and fully man. It teaches that the preincarnate Word, the eternal Son of God, took upon himself actual humanity and became a unique person. A person with a unique and complicated nature. If God were to become a man, we would expect many complexities and difficult questions about His nature. This is the kind of picture we find painted of Jesus in the Bible.

Reviewing Chapter 4 would help you to better answer errors (see also Phil. 2:5–11, John 17:1–5, and Heb. 2:9–18).

Deviating from the Simultaneous Existence of Three Persons

Similar to changing three persons to one person, this error is caused by overemphasis on the oneness of God. However, instead of denying the equality of the persons, this deviation denies the simultaneous existence of the persons.

This deviation has roots in an early Christian heresy called either *modalism, monarchianism,* or *Sabelianism* (after Sabelius who first espoused this view). This perspective contends that there is one God and one person. He has either manifested himself in different ways or modes at different times, or has wrongly had many different titles ascribed to Him.

William Marrion Branham and his present followers espouse this view. They are an example of a larger group often identified as "Jesus Only" churches. The term "Jesus Only" comes from their baptismal ritual in which they baptize in the name of Jesus only, not in the name of the Father, of the Son, and of the Holy Spirit.

Branham writes:

> How can three persons be in one God? Not only is there no Bible for it, but it shows even a lack of intelligent reasoning. Three distinct persons, though identical substance, make three gods, or language has lost its meaning entirely.[10]

> It is not that there are three Gods, but one God with three offices. There is ONE God with three titles, Father, Son, and Holy Ghost.[11]

> The Jehovah of the Old Testament is the Jesus of the New. No matter how hard you try, you can't prove there are THREE Gods. But it also takes a revelation by the Holy Spirit to make you understand the truth that He is One. It takes a revelation to see that the Jehovah of the Old Testament is the Jesus of the New. Satan crept into the church and blinded the people to this truth.[12]

Often these "Jesus Only" groups indict orthodox Christians as *tritheists*, believers in three gods. This is a poor rendering of the orthodox position on the Trinity. The problem with modalism, of course, is the eternal existence of three persons and their social interaction among each other.

Several scripture texts are used to argue this view. The first is John 10:30: "I and the Father are one."

It appears that Jesus is saying that He is the same person as the Father. However, this is not the case. There are three forms of this word for "one" in the Greek: "heis," "mia," and "hen." "Heis" is masculine, "mia" is feminine, and "hen" is neuter.

When one wishes to demonstrate that a title refers to one person, then "heis" or "mia" is used. The neuter "hen" carries the idea of purpose, two things of one purpose. "Hen" is used

---

[10]William Marrion Branham, *An Exposition of the Seven Church Ages* (Tucson, Ariz.), p. 18.
[11]Branham, ibid., p. 18.
[12]Branham, ibid., p. 26.

in John 10:30. It is simply saying that Jesus and the Father are of one nature and purpose, enough of a statement in and of itself to be considered blasphemy by the Jews. This use of "hen" can also be seen in 1 Cor. 3:8.

> Now he who plants and he who waters are one; but each will receive his own reward according to his own labor. (NASB)

The context clearly teaches that two people are referred to, the planter and the waterer. Nevertheless, both are one in purpose.

A second passage often developed to demonstrate modalism is John 14:8–9.

> Philip said, "Lord, show us the Father and that will be enough for us." Jesus answered: "Don't you know me, Philip, even after I have been among you such a long time? Anyone who has seen me has seen the Father. How can you say, 'Show us the Father'?"

Is Jesus saying that He is the person of the Father? We can be sure He did not mean that. John, the apostle who recorded these verses, also wrote in the first chapter of his gospel that the Son revealed the Father to us.

> The Word became flesh and lived for a while among us. We have seen his glory, the glory of the one and only Son, who came from the Father, full of grace and truth. No one has ever seen God, but God the only Son, who is at the Father's side, has made him known. (John 1:14, 18)

Jesus manifested and revealed the invisible God. To see Jesus is to see the Father (Heb. 1:1–3; Col. 1:15).

Another passage often cited to illustrate the basis of this error is Isa. 9:6. "For to us a child is born, to us a son will be given, and the government will be on His shoulders. And he will be called Wonderful Counselor, Mighty God, Everlasting Father, Prince of Peace."

Again, it appears that the coming Messiah is also the Everlasting Father. Since Old Testament names illustrate character, one would assume the title "Everlasting Father" refers to Jesus.

However, the translation of this Hebrew construction can be misleading. These two words are in a form known as a *construct*. A literal translation of the phrase would be "Father of eternity." Generally, all Hebrew constructs are translated as a noun and an adjective, for example, "everlasting Father." However, the nuance of the meaning is that the Messiah is the Father, or the begetter, of Eternity.[13]

The last chapter provided the biblical basis for denying the false doctrine of modalism, the idea that the one God has manifested himself in different ways. However, I will note one scripture that emphasizes the distinctiveness of the persons.

> "Therefore go and make disciples of all nations, baptizing them in the name of the Father and of the Son and of the Holy Spirit, and teaching them to obey everything I have commanded you. And surely I will be with you always, to the very end of the age." (Matt. 28:19–20)

In these verses, the repetition of two kinds of words lends support to the doctrine of the three persons. The grammatical rule we used to decipher John 1:1 also applies to these verses. That rule, which you can find in the Appendix, helps us understand that the *the*'s and *and*'s are in the text to give emphasis and show unity among the Father, Son, and Holy Spirit. "The" (*tou*) is used with each title, and each title is separated by "and" (*kaî*). This lends authority for the view that three distinct individuals are referred to in this context.

> . . . in the name of *the* (*tou*) Father *and the* (*kai tou*) Son, *and the* (*kai tou*) Holy Spirit.

If one person were to be referred to, the Greek would more likely read:

> . . . in the name of *the* Father, Son, *and* Holy Spirit.

Or,

> In the name of *the* Father, *the* Son, and *the* Holy Spirit.

We do not wish to force our grammatical rule into saying too much, but given the other possible constructions and the fact that each title has both the article and its own conjunction, it seems that three persons would be the most likely meaning of these verses.

---

[13]For further discussion see: *Encyclopedia of Bible Difficulties*, Gleason Archer (Grand Rapids: Mich.: Zondervan, 1982), p. 268.

Deviating from the Personal Nature of the Godhead

Several New Testament epistles appear to be responses to a philosophy that later matured into what we call *gnosticism*. Attempting to make a complicated philosophy simple, we can say that one of the tenets of gnosticism that relates to the Trinity is the distinction it draws between that which is physical, and therefore evil, and that which is spiritual, and therefore pure. This is particularly relevant to the person of Jesus Christ. A distinction was drawn between Jesus, the physical man, and Jesus, the spiritual Christ.

Naturally, the source of this deviation in the early church was new congregations in areas saturated with Greek philosophy. A mixture of these philosophies and Christian doctrine began to merge, causing the early gnostic heresy.

Today also there are Christian Gnostics who alter the definition of the Trinity by changing the meaning of "person" to a more spiritual concept. Christian Science as well as the Unity School of Christianity are examples of Gnostic cults.

Christian Science says:

> The theory of three persons in one God (that is, a personal Trinity or Tri-unity) suggests polytheism, rather than one ever-present I Am.[14]

> Jesus. The highest human corporeal concept of the divine idea, rebuking and destroying error and bringing to light man's immortality.[15]

Unity says:

> The Father is Principle, the Son is that Principle revealed in the creative plan, the Holy Spirit is the executive power of both.[16]

> God is not a . . . person, having life, intelligence, love, or power. God is that invisible, intangible, but very real something we call life.[17]

---

[14]Mary Baker Eddy, *Science and Health with Key to the Scriptures* (Boston, Mass.: The First Church of Christ, Scientist, 1971), p. 256.

[15]Eddy, ibid., glossary, p. 589.

[16]Walter Martin, *The Kingdom of the Cults* (Minneapolis, Minn.: Bethany House Publishers, 1965), p. 279. (Quoted from *Metaphysical Bible Dictionary*, Unity School of Christianity, p. 629.)

[17]Martin, ibid., p. 279. (Quoted from *Lessons in Truth*, H. Emily Cady, Kansas City: Unity School of Christianity, 1925, p. 6).

When evaluating the alleged biblical basis for Gnostic doctrines, it becomes clear that the issue has really shifted from doctrine to the way that Scripture is interpreted. Just as the Gnostic cultist will spiritualize the concept of Christ, he will spiritualize the words of the Bible.

For example, a Gnostic cultist may cite Rom. 8:5–9 and use this text to show that there is a physical level, and a spiritual-mystical level. However, context itself makes clear that this is not the meaning of the text. They would contend that our inability to see that deeper level of meaning is proof that we are on the physical level.

We will not resolve this conflict now because it relates mostly to interpretation. Instead, we will discuss it later within the context of authority. For now, we can at least recognize that Gnostic cults change the meaning of "person" by viewing the persons of the Father, the Christ, and the Spirit in such a way as to draw a division between the person and a spiritualized concept. "Yes," they would contend, "Jesus is a person, but Christ is not. Christ is a perspective or principle."

Since the apostles responded to early forms of this deviation, their responses are very important. Paul said that "in Christ all the fullness of Deity lives in bodily form" (Col. 2:9).

The Apostle John did not see the need to separate the physical body of Jesus from the Christ. Quite the contrary, he demanded that they must be viewed as one.

> This is how you can recognize the Spirit of God: Every spirit that acknowledges that Jesus Christ has come in the flesh is from God, but every spirit that does not acknowledge Jesus is not from God. This is the spirit of the antichrist, which you have heard is coming and even now is already in the world. (1 John 4:2–3)

Another fashion in which the meaning of "person" has been changed is the result of the influx of pantheistic theologies. Many cults today are flourishing because America is flirting with Eastern philosophies and various forms of Hinduism. You probably know someone who has toyed with meditation. When people attempt to meditate in such a way as to empty their mind or achieve some sort of special consciousness, they are adopting a form of Hinduism.

Hindu philosophy teaches that all physical matter is a lower form of God. Consequently, God is everything. Taking the Greek words for "everything" (*pan*) and God (*theos*) we get the term *pantheism*. By attempting to gain consciousness or harmony with nature, meditators are attempting to recognize that they are really part of God, attempting to find *God consciousness*. This is not Christian meditation. The biblical God is a personal being who transcends human frailties. The god of a monistic, Eastern world view, is not transcendent or personal. In this view, we have a denial of the persons of the Trinity.

EST, Erhard Seminars Training, is one of the current groups with Hindu foundations. The philosophy of EST says, "In actuality, each of us, as the sole creator of our universe, is a God . . . 'You are God and you create everything around you and you create the universe.' And, 'You are in effect recognizing your own Godhood.' "[18]

Transcendental meditation is another example of this Eastern perspective. TM, although claiming to be only science and technique, appears in reality to dabble in theology. Maharishi Mahesh Yogi declares, "Although we are all 100% Divine, . . . consciously we do not know that we are Divine, so there is no connection, there is no bridge and we suffer on the conscious level."[19]

The simplest refutation of the depersonalization of the members of the Trinity is in the person of Christ. He is fully God, and definitely person.

> In the beginning was the Word and the Word was with God, and the Word was God. The Word became flesh and lived for a while among us. We have seen his glory, the glory of the one and only Son, who came from the Father, full of grace and truth. (John 1:1, 14)

---

[18]John Weldon, *A Guide to Cults and New Religions* (Downers Grove, Ill.: Inter-Varsity Press, 1983). Three quotes taken from: Rhinehart, *Book of est*, pp. 216–217; Donald Porter and Diane Taxson, *The est Experience*, New York, Award Books, 1976, p. 101; ibid., p. 212, p. 86.

[19]Pat Means, *The Mystical Maze* (San Bernardino, Calif.: Campus Crusade for Christ, 1976), pp. 138–139. (Quoted from *Meditations of Maharishi Mahesh Yogi*, Maharishi Mahesh Yogi, Bantam Books, 1973.)

Conclusion

It might be puzzling after an extended discussion about the Trinity that I would personally *not* recommend that you discuss this doctrine at great length with a cultist. A vast majority of the times in which I have begun a discussion with a Jehovah's Witness, *they* have tried to bring up the Trinity. Each time, I mentioned that I had reservations about whom they believed Jesus was, and they would respond with confident enthusiasm, "Oh, you mean the Trinity."

"No," I responded, "I mean the person of Jesus Christ."

"Yes, you are referring to the doctrine of the Trinity," they would continue.

Again I reaffirmed, "No, I am concerned with your definition of Jesus Christ. If I am wrong about who he is, then I *am* wrong about the Trinity. But if you are wrong on who He is, then you do not know Jehovah."

The reason they want to discuss the Trinity is that it is so complex. Being complex does not make the doctrine of the Trinity untrue, but it does make it a literal haven for a vast number of rehearsed questions and arguments. To understand the doctrine of the Trinity, the individual must first be open-minded and teachable. Those two traits do not usually characterize a cultist in a debate about the Trinity. The Jehovah's Witnesses would love to get into a discussion about human reason, the Scriptures, and the Holy Spirit. But it would not be productive for you to dwell on those issues which detract from the strong evidence for the deity of Christ.

I would suggest delving into the Trinity only when it is absolutely essential. Even then, discuss only those particular elements which are relevant for the particular cult you are dealing with. For example, an individual who is involved in a "Jesus Only" group will be delighted with your presentation on the deity of Christ. However, it will be necessary to discuss the element of plurality with this individual.

Nevertheless, the bedrock of Christian belief, the deity of Christ, must be the foundational platform for discussing any other point of doctrine.

Study Questions for Part II

1. What is the Trinity?
2. What are the essential elements in the definition of the Trinity?
3. Why is the doctrine of the Trinity confusing?
4. What can't we understand about the doctrine of the Trinity?
5. What is the basis for the Trinity doctrine?
6. What is the relationship of reason to the doctrine of the Trinity?
7. What is a *biblical mystery*?
8. What is *selective biblicity* and its relationship to the doctrine of the Trinity?
9. Which texts demonstrate the oneness of God?
10. Which texts demonstrate the plurality of God?
11. What does the Bible teach about God the Father?
12. What does the Bible teach about God the Son?
13. What does the Bible teach about God the Holy Spirit?
14. What does the Bible teach about the relationship between the three persons?
15. How and why do some cults deviate from the oneness of God?
16. How and why do some cults deviate from the plurality of the Godhead?
17. How and why do some cults deviate from the existence of the three persons?
18. How and why do some cults change the concept of plurality?

PART III

Salvation

◆ 8 ◆

God's Gift of Salvation

Your father probably told you, "Anything worth having is worth working for," or, "That which comes too easily is too lightly esteemed." We all know that you get what you pay for.

Nevertheless, we believe in God's free gift, salvation by grace through faith. Can we really trust a theology which can extravagantly claim that salvation is a free gift? Salvation seems to be simple and easy, but it is far from being without great value.

One of the important implications of God creating mankind in the fashion that He did is that He could relate to mankind in a personal way. When Adam and Eve fell into sin in the garden, that intimate, personal fellowship was seriously affected. As a result, mankind throughout history has seen the necessity of rectifying its relationship with God. So man invented ways of doing just that.

The basic goal of all religions is to bring man and God back together. But not all religions are equal. The crucial question is, *How* do they get God and man back on speaking terms? The answer to that question will reveal whether God or man invented that particular religious system.

The Perfect Demand

God is holy. His holy nature demands holiness in those with whom He is to have a personal relationship. As a result, we read the admonition that men ought to be holy because God is holy (1 Pet. 1:15, 16). To avoid the problem of man inventing his own system of holiness, God clearly defined the demands of holiness in the hundreds of rules, laws, and ordinances which comprise the Old Testament law.

But unlike a math exam, there is no partial credit. The demands of the law are perfection. God's standard is a pass or fail, a credit or noncredit proposition. Even before the law of Moses, God's demands were high. For example, He demanded a blameless life of Abraham.

> When Abram was ninety-nine years old, the Lord appeared to him and said, "I am God Almighty; Walk before me and be blameless." (Gen. 17:1)

The Apostle Paul in the epistle to the Galatians quotes the law from Deut. 27:26 when he says, "Cursed is everyone who does not continue to do everything written in the Book of the Law" (Gal. 3:10).

James in his epistle provides the clearest statement as to the unequivocation of the demands of the law, "For whoever keeps the whole law and yet stumbles at just one point is guilty of breaking all of it" (James 2:10). This may sound very strict, even legalistic, but with good reason.

If we wish to know God, then we must meet God on His terms. God cannot compromise His character. He judges us on the basis of His nature, not ours. God demands perfection, and if we wish to know Him, we must be perfect.

The Imperfect Response

No man is perfect by works of the law. When painting, white paint is kept pure only by mixing it with more white paint. If any other color is mixed with white, no matter how close it may be, it will darken the white's purity. Certainly God is not paint, but this illustrates why a holy God cannot even associate with evil.

While I was answering questions, after speaking in a dorm one evening, a student responded, "That's not fair! Nobody's perfect." I had to agree with part of what he said; man is not perfect. That is what the Bible has always said. Paul described the behavior of the Ephesians before they came to know Christ:

> . . . in which you used to live when you followed the ways of this world and of the ruler of the kingdom of the air, the spirit who is now at work in those who are disobedient. All of us also lived among them at one time, gratifying the cravings of our sinful

nature and following its desires and thoughts. Like the rest, we were by nature objects of wrath. (Eph. 2:2–3)

Similarly, Paul wrote to the Romans:

> As it is written: "There is no one righteous, no even one; there is no one who understands, no one who seeks God. All have turned away, they have together become worthless; there is no one who does good, not even one." (Rom. 3:10–12)

As a result of the demands of God's law and our rebellion, it is no surprise that all of us have failed to meet the standard of perfection that God has instituted. Paul's statement stands: "For all have sinned and fall short of the glory of God" (Rom. 3:23).

How can God be just in condemning us if we have all sinned? After all, everyone does it? The question is better stated: "Is God justified in condemning us for being unholy?" A holy God could do no less and still be holy. If God does not judge sin, He himself would be capricious, an unjust judge who makes exceptions.

To maintain justice, God must consistently exercise His justice. Which is more just, for God to pass judgment on all sin and on every sinner, or to make exceptions for some sins and certain sinners? The answer is obvious. It would not be fair for a judge to make exceptions for some, but not for others.

If men are doomed to fail in fulfilling the law, then what is its purpose? Paul gives two good reasons for the law. First, our failure in performing the law demonstrates that we have certainly sinned and are, therefore, accountable before God.

> Now we know that whatever the law says, it says to those who are under the law, so that every mouth may be silenced and the whole world held accountable to God. Therefore no one will be declared righteous in his sight by observing the law; rather, through the law we became conscious of sin. (Rom. 3:19–20)

Second, when we compare our seemingly perfect conduct and lives to God's perfect standard, we understand that we all fall short. This recognition that man is unable to meet the demands of the law should motivate man to see the need for a Savior.

> So the law was put in charge to lead us to Christ, that we might be justified by faith. (Gal. 3:24)

This idea is not popular in our culture, either. It is often expressed that man needs no one and is accountable to no one.

Yet, the law shows us that we are accountable to God for our sinfulness and that we need salvation.

The Perfect Solution

God is holy and demands holiness. God is also just and His justice allows no exceptions, even though no man is able to meet the demands of the law. But God still loves mankind. This presents us with a quandry. How can all three attributes be balanced?

Generally, when mankind attempts to resolve this tension, he denies at least one of the three attributes. Either God becomes holy and loving and, therefore, makes exceptions: "How could a loving God send people to hell?" Or He becomes holy and just, but not loving. Or, He becomes loving and just without being holy. Can we resolve this tension?

The solution is a holy and just savior who perfectly fulfills the law for us. Jesus, being God, was able to be perfect (Heb. 5:9). Therefore, He came to earth to fulfill the law. As discussed in Chapter 4, Matt. 5:17–20 quotes Jesus as He discusses His relationship to the law. Jesus did not come to abolish the law, but to fulfill both the law and the prophets. However, He did not come to fulfill it in His role as God, but as man. As a result, the New Testament portrays Jesus not only as the Son of God, God come in the flesh, but also as the Son of Man.

Jesus the Man

As the Son of Man, Jesus was able to fulfill specific responsibilities.

> Since the children have flesh and blood, he too shared in their humanity so that by his death he might destroy him who holds the power of death—that is, the devil—and free those who all their lives were held in slavery by their fear of death. For surely it is not angels he helps, but Abraham's descendants. (Heb. 2:14–16)

Jesus was to become a man so that He would be able to identify with His human brothers and make propitiation for sins. Before Jesus could make propitiation for sins, He had to live a life qualifying Him to be an appropriate sacrifice for sins. Simply,

He had to live a perfect life and fulfill the law.

We see this from the beginning of Jesus' ministry to the end. Matt. 3:13–15 speaks of the baptism of Jesus. John the Baptist recognized the authority of Christ and hesitated to baptize him. Even so, notice the response of Jesus. "Let it be so now; it is proper for us to do this to fulfill all righteousness" (Matt. 3:15).

Throughout Jesus' ministry, He lived under the authority of God the Father and the regulations of the law. Jesus could not sin and still redeem mankind. Therefore, even though He was God in human form, He could only do that which was in accordance with the Father's will, submitting to the Father's authority as any man. "And being found in appearance as a man, he humbled himself and became obedient to death—even death on a cross!" (Phil. 2:8). This obedience extended all the way to the cross, where even the death of Jesus was in accordance with the law.

Jesus the Cursed

Heb. 9:22 demonstrates that there is no forgiveness without the shedding of blood. "In fact, the law requires that nearly everything be cleansed with blood, and without the shedding of blood there is no forgiveness."

Note especially that the basis for the death of Christ was the law. In John 19:7, the Jews demanded the death of Jesus because Jesus claimed to be the Son of God. This is usually blasphemy. If a man claimed to be God, he would be lying and deserving of death, unless the claim were true! Jesus was not committing blasphemy. He was telling the truth. Nevertheless, the law stated that *anyone* claiming such was to die. Recognize the impact of this: God gave the law and included himself in the judgment for blasphemy. When God set this penalty, did He know that Jesus would claim to be the Son of God? Yes. Jesus planned His own judgment.

It is clear that none of this drama was by chance. It was planned by God. "This Man, was handed over to you by God's set purpose and foreknowledge; and you, with the help of wicked men, put him to death by nailing him to the cross" (Acts 2:23).

The law states that any man that hangs on a tree is under

God's curse (Deut. 21:23). The Jews did not hang people as a form of capital punishment. After death, the corpses were sometimes hung as a public warning, but only after death. However, at the time of Christ, the Roman Empire was in control of Israel. They outlawed capital punishment by local authorities and punished the guilty with their own form of capital punishment: crucifixion. Quite appropriately, in the fullness of time, Christ was born. God sovereignly organized His own death and curse, yet, without sinning. Sin was imputed upon Christ when He was cursed by hanging on a tree.

Jesus the Sacrifice

Consequently, Christ was our substitute. In Gal. 3:13, Paul makes this clear. "Christ redeemed us from the curse of the law by becoming a curse for us, for it is written: 'Cursed is everyone who is hung on a tree.'" In 1 Cor. 15:3, Paul notes that the core of the gospel is that Christ died for our sins, *according to the Scriptures.*

One of the scriptures Paul was referring to is found in Isaiah 53. In this prophecy about the suffering servant, one issue becomes very clear: He was to be a substitute for sins.

> Surely he took up our infirmities and carried our sorrows, yet we considered him stricken by God, smitten by him, and afflicted. But he was pierced for our transgressions, he was crushed for our iniquities; the punishment that brought us peace was upon him, and by his wounds we are healed. We all, like sheep, have gone astray, each of us has turned to his own way; and the Lord has laid on him the iniquity of us all. (Isa. 53:4–6)

The results of this plan are clear, the way of salvation has been completed by Christ. Peter, in his first epistle, not only declares that Jesus died for sins, but that He finished it.

> For Christ died for sins once and for all, the righteous for the unrighteous, to bring you to God. He was put to death in the body but made alive by the Spirit. (1 Pet. 3:18)

Jesus was a perfect sacrifice, sinless, holy, and righteous, because he had fulfilled the law.

> God made him who had no sin to be sin for us, so that in him

we might become the righteousness of God. (2 Cor. 5:21)

The author of Hebrews demonstrates the finality of the sacrifice of Jesus.

> And by that will, we have been made holy through the sacrifice of the body of Jesus Christ once for all. Day after day every priest stands and performs his religious duties; again and again he offers the same sacrifices, which can never take away sins. But when this priest had offered for all time one sacrifice for sins, he sat down at the right hand of God. Since that time he waits for his enemies to be made a footstool, because by one sacrifice he has made perfect forever those who are being made holy. (Heb. 10:10–14)

Has God maintained His holy standard? Has He denied His justice? Is His love compromised? No! "But God demonstrates his own love for us in this: While we were still sinners, Christ died for us" (Rom. 5:8).

The Meaning of Salvation

Salvation is not man attempting to reach God by living a life good enough. It is God coming down to man, taking the form of a man, and fulfilling the law for us.

Since it was Jesus coming down to us, living a perfect life, and then dying in our place, what is our responsibility in salvation? As any sacrifice under the Old Testament law, we must identify with it. John, in the first chapter of his gospel, said, "Yet to all who received him, to those who believed in his name he gave the right to become children of God" (John 1:12).

The responsibility of man is to believe in Christ, exercise faith, and receive what Christ has made available. Salvation is a free gift to be accepted, not a wage to be earned.

◆9◆

By Grace or Works

The scene was common on TV in almost every home throughout the United States. The family sat down to a supper of steaming vegetables, melting butter over mounds of mashed potatoes, and a neat plate of crunchy, golden-fried chicken. The camera zoomed in on a cute little girl with a distinctive accent who said, "It's not frah'd, it's Shake and Bake, and ah hailp'd!"

This vignette has been reproduced in a number of homes with varying degrees of local color and accent. A small child has been joyfully dodging Mom's knees in the kitchen. This little ankle biter somehow participates in the process of fixing dinner. At the table, with beaming eyes and considerable pride, the final proclamation is made, "And I helped!"

We human beings take considerable satisfaction and pride in those things we help to accomplish. The only greater sense of pride comes from accomplishing something alone. Proud toddlers who tie their shoes or comb their hair for the first time gleefully declare, "I did it all by myself!"

Unfortunately, this deeply engraved mentality often surfaces in relationship to salvation, the gift of God. The greater our sins, the greater God's grace. The less we can do, the greater God's glory. In Romans, chapter 4, while discussing the relationship of works and circumcision to salvation, Paul said:

> Now when a man works, his wages are not credited to him as a gift, but as an obligation. However, to the man who does not work but trusts God who justifies the wicked, his faith is credited as righteousness. David says the same thing when he speaks of the blessedness of the man to whom God credits righteousness apart from works: "Blessed are they whose transgressions are forgiven, whose sins are covered." (Rom. 4:4–7)

Salvation is from the Lord, and He is glorified by extending grace to men. This is why God takes men who were spiritually dead and makes them alive: "In order that in the coming ages He might show the incomparable riches of his grace, expressed in kindness to us in Christ Jesus" (Eph. 2:7).

However, men want to say, "I helped." But what is man able to do? No matter what part man plays in earning salvation, he must do it perfectly. Consequently, salvation is solely through Christ, and this is to God's great glory! Jesus came to earth. Jesus lived a perfect life. Jesus died on the cross for sins. Jesus rose from the dead. Somehow, man jumping onto the stage attempting to share the spotlight with Christ, saying, "And I helped," seems wholly out of place. We cannot earn our salvation by works.

The classic text on the relationship of works and the gift of salvation is Eph. 2:8–9:

> For it is by grace you have been saved, through faith—and this not from yourselves, it is the gift of God—not by works, so that no one can boast.

We see that salvation is a gift of God, based upon His grace, and received through our faith, not on the basis of our works. Good works are a result of salvation, but not a means to it.

In Paul's epistle to Titus, he makes clear the relationship of salvation and works:

> He saved us, not because of righteous things we had done, but because of his mercy. He saved us through the washing of re-birth and renewal by the Holy Spirit, whom he poured out on us generously through Jesus Christ our Savior, so that having been justified by his grace, we might become heirs having the hope of eternal life. This is a trustworthy saying. And I want you to stress these things, so that those who have trusted in God may be careful to devote themselves to doing what is good. These things are excellent and profitable for everyone. (Titus 3:5–8)

The reason for this relationship is clear. The demands of the law are perfection. Man can neither live perfectly nor earn his salvation. That is why Christ came to do it for us. If men could earn their salvation, the incarnation and death of Christ were unnecessary. If man were responsible for even part of the works necessary for salvation, his part would have to be perfect. But if man were responsible for only one percent, he would fail even

in that one percent. Like a chain with a hundred percent links:
If man's righteousness were only one link, the chain would still
break.

In our culture, we hurt our pride by depending solely upon
Jesus for salvation, because it requires humility and submission.
We want to feel that we have had a part, that we have done
something to help earn our eternal life. Salvation gives no
ground for man to boast. It is a free gift, but definitely not cheap;
the Son of God shed His blood that we might obtain eternal life.

Salvation by Works

Most cults add personal works as a necessity for salvation.
Mormons exemplify this perspective.

> In addition to this redemption from death, all men, by the grace
> of God, have the power to gain eternal life. This is called sal-
> vation by grace coupled with obedience to the laws and ordi-
> nances of the gospel.[1]

> Christians speak often of the blood of Christ and its cleansing
> power. Much that is believed and taught on this subject, how-
> ever, is such utter nonsense and so palpably false that to believe
> it is to lose one's salvation. Many go so far, for instance, as to
> pretend, at least, to believe that if we confess Christ with our
> lips and avow that we accept him as our personal Savior, we are
> thereby saved. His blood, without other act than mere belief,
> they say, makes us clean. . . .[2]

> But there are certain conditions attached to the attainment of
> salvation through his atoning blood.[3]

Armstrong also denies salvation on the basis of faith alone
with no works.

> Notice that Peter did NOT say their sins would be blotted out
> immediately upon this repentance. Belief alone in the atoning
> DEATH of Christ does not completely change or convert
> one. . . .

> So we humans are not finally SAVED by the BLOOD of Christ;

---

[1]*What the Mormons Think of Christ* (Salt Lake City: The Church of Jesus Christ of
Latter-day Saints, Deseret Press), p. 28.
[2]*What the Mormons Think of Christ*, ibid., p. 31.
[3]*What the Mormons Think of Christ*, ibid., p. 32.

we are restored to contact with God, who has eternal life to GIVE.[4]

It is necessary to make this explanation, at this point, because the popular deception of a deceived traditional "Christianity" is to claim that when one "receives Christ"—"accepts Christ"—"professes Christ"—or first receives God's Holy Spirit to dwell in him, that he is already "BORN AGAIN."[5]

Certainly Jesus didn't overlook faith, or grace, or belief, or the efficacy in His name!

Yet despite that, Jesus said instead: "If you will enter into life, KEEP THE COMMANDMENTS"![6]

Whenever a group insists that Christ's death on the cross was not sufficient in and of itself for the salvation of men, and that works or rituals of any sort must be added to faith, the gospel has been altered. Paul, when writing to the church in Galatia, rebuked those who wished to add works, specifically the ritual of circumcision, to salvation.

I am astonished that you are so quickly deserting the one who called you by the grace of Christ and are turning to a different gospel—which is really no gospel at all. Evidently some people are throwing you into confusion and are trying to pervert the gospel of Christ. You foolish Galatians! Who has bewitched you? (Gal. 1:6–7; 3:1)

In contrast, Paul constantly refers to faith in Christ's work on the cross as the basis of salvation.

Know that a man is not justified by observing the law, but by faith in Jesus Christ. So we, too, have put our faith in Christ and not by observing the law, because by observing the law no one will be justified. I would like to learn just one thing from you: Did you receive the Spirit by observing the law, or by believing what you heard? You are all sons of God through faith in Christ Jesus. (Gal. 2:16; 3:2, 26)

Now, it is important to draw a distinction here between working to earn one's salvation, and the fruit of perseverance. Some

---

[4]Herbert W. Armstrong, "What is Uppermost in God's Mind?", *The Plain Truth*, July 1977, p. 3.

[5]Herbert W. Armstrong, "Just What Do You Mean: Born Again?", *The Plain Truth*, February 1977, pp. 30–31.

[6]Jon Hill, "What Can You Do to Get Eternal Life?", *The Plain Truth*, October-November 1977, p. 29.

falsely contend that believers from traditional Wesleyan/Arminian churches espouse salvation by works because they believe that salvation can be lost.

However, to say such is to falsely present the Wesleyan point of view and to change some definitions, which create straw men. Those of the Wesleyan position agree that man is saved solely through the work of Christ on the cross, and that works are of no value. However, they contend that if a person stops believing, that he can lose his salvation. This is not works salvation. There is a significant difference between this view and the views of works advanced by cults. To imply that this is cultic salvation by works is to contend that faith is a work. This is not the perspective of either the Wesleyans or the New Testament. It is merely a convenient, oversimplified argument.

Wesleyans expect fruit in the life of the true believer. When someone becomes a new creation in Christ Jesus (2 Cor. 5:17) and the Holy Spirit indwells him (Rom. 8:9), then this new nature would be expected to produce fruit (Gal. 5:22). The New Testament abounds with the teaching that he who practices sin is of the devil (1 John 3:7–8). It is not works salvation to expect the new convert to begin to practice holiness because God is holy (1 Pet. 1:15). And we do not teach works salvation by confronting a believer if he persists in walking in sin.

To contend that this is salvation by works demonstrates an undue fear of works salvation and forces us to manipulate the Scripture to maintain the position. There is no need to fear. Scripture clearly communicates balance. We need not be either legalistic or hesistant to expect fruit. The Lord fulfills His responsibility to conform the believer into the image of Christ, "Being confident of this that he who began a good work in you will carry it on to completion until the day of Christ Jesus" (Phil. 1:6).

Salvation by Faith in the Leader

The second way cults alter salvation is by changing the object of faith from Jesus, who is our substitute, to another individual. Sometimes this switching can be difficult to detect. Jim Jones was an example of this perspective. He became "Father," the object of his adherents' faith.

William Marrion Branham often said, as most cultists do, that we must have faith in Christ. This appears orthodox, but in reality is quite deceptive. For as one studies Branham further, one begins to see that faith in Christ is secondary to faith in Branham.

This is an important issue to understand. Branham, as many other false prophets, said emphatically that one is saved on the basis of grace through faith. Yet, Branham believed that people who are never born again by faith in Jesus Christ will have eternal life.

> We will actually show by Scripture that multitudes who were not even born again will go into eternal life. As strange as that may sound, it is certainly true.[7]

> But upon what grounds do they enter into life eternal? Certainly not upon the fact that they already have His life as does the bride, but they receive it because they were kind to His brethren. They are not His brethren: that would make them joint-heirs with Jesus. . . . Now because of their love of the people of God they are recognized and saved.[8]

And what will happen to the orthodox Christian church who do not honor Branham?

> But whose names did not remain? Those of the world system churches who fought the bride will be those whose names are removed. That is who will lose out. They will be cast into the lake of fire.[9]

Did you catch that? After Branham says many times that we are saved only through Jesus Christ, he becomes the real source of salvation. Those with faith in Branham and those friendly to him, even if they do not have faith in Christ, will receive eternal life. Those Christians who have only faith in Christ, but not in Branham, will be damned. Salvation has deceptively been changed.

---

[7] William Marrion Branham, *An Exposition of the Seven Church Ages* (Tucson, Ariz.), p. 266.

[8] William Marrion Branham, ibid., p. 278.

[9] William Marrion Branham, ibid., p. 279.

Salvation by God Consciousness

In some cases, the ardent devotion shown to a guru or mystical teacher can be similar. When we begin to discuss this kind of cult, we have shifted to another world view: Eastern philosophy. In these cults, the shifting of faith is obvious. Someone in an Eastern cult would not place his faith in Christ simply because the concept of the cross holds a traditional Christian meaning. He has little concern about Christian traditions. Nevertheless, he may say that his guru is another manifestation of the Universal Soul, just as Jesus was a manifestation to His culture.

Even so, the way that Eastern cults often alter biblical salvation has to do with the concept of sin rather than the person they follow. Although they may see their guru as being a god, to them salvation comes from following his method, not by placing faith vicariously in the teacher. This leads us to the third way salvation can be altered.

Some cults, mostly those based upon the Eastern mind-set, change salvation by denying the unbridgeable gap between God and man. They argue that there is no gap between God and man due to sin because we are all a part of the divine essence. The only gap is our ignorance of our divinity. Therefore, the goal of the individual is to develop his personal God consciousness.

Historically, works salvation has been preached by heretics ever since the time of Christ. While works salvation is still very much a problem, our current culture is seeing the rapid and expansive growth of the Eastern mind-set in many subtle areas. I believe this is the realm where the greatest amount of deviation will take place in the future. The vast number of self-help groups and forms of meditation as well as the growth of the occult, all stressing opening yourself up to experiential encounters with a greater "force" give testimony to this. People are intrigued today with mysticism and experience. They want to experience power, special knowledge, or develop unique abilities. People in our strongly technical society want to see and use the supernatural.

Oddly enough, a technical, scientific world is eager to accept the supernatural if it can be couched in scientific terminology (such as "parapsychology") and described as the natural, untapped abilities of our minds. Seminars abound on various Eastern and occultic practices dressed up with self-help human potential, and inner peace jargon.

A pseudo-Christian cult, Christian Science, alters salvation similar to the Eastern cults. Gnostic in nature, they believe the world of Christianity is a world of illusion, especially in regard to salvation. They emphasize that man does not really need salvation. "We see that man has never lost his spiritual estate and his eternal harmony."[10] This can be true because evil is also an illusion. "Hence, evil is but an illusion, and it has no real basis. Evil is a false belief."[11] Of what effect was Jesus' death on the cross?

> The material blood of Jesus was no more efficacious to cleanse from sin when it was shed upon "the accursed tree," than when it was flowing in his veins as he went daily about his Father's business.[12]

> Final deliverance from error, whereby we rejoice in immortality, boundless freedom, and sinless sense, is not reached through paths of flowers nor by pinning one's faith without works to another's vicarious effort.[13]

According to Christian Science, then, salvation comes with the realization that the material world does not exist. We are to live in the spiritual realm and ignore the myths of sin and pain.

Salvation by Unity

The ecumenical movement has pushed for unity across denominational lines. Liberal ecumenists have tried to meld Christian beliefs with those of other religions. Any such attempt at unity leaves us without anything firmer than *universalism*, the idea that God will save all men.

The results? Christ's substitutionary death upon the cross is no longer a basis for faith, but an unnecessary dogma. Theology

---

[10]Mary Baker Eddy, *Science and Health with Key to the Scriptures* (Boston, Mass.: The First Church of Christ, Scientist, 1971), p. 548.
[11]Eddy, ibid., p. 480.
[12]Eddy, ibid., p. 25.
[13]Eddy, ibid., p. 22.

sees no distinction between the faith of the Christian Church, the cult, or any other religion.

Let me illustrate this trend by noting the direction of one established denomination. In seeking to establish unity among the differing faiths of various groups, and accepting the premise that truth is relative rather than written revelation from God, they have eliminated any doctrinal basis for fellowship with Christians. Claiming to follow only Christ, they have denied much of what Jesus taught.

> We believe in the living Christ at work in the heart of the individual believer. We believe in tolerance of another's point of view and in respect for the sincere conviction of every human being. We think and let think. The Community Church recognizes in the historic creeds progressive efforts to put into words the meaning of God's eternal truth revealed in Jesus Christ. It does not, however ascribe finality or infallibility to any human dogma.[14]

This sounds fairly appealing until one sees this philosophy applied.

> We have not been and cannot become a creedal movement in the sense that there will be a set of beliefs to which an individual must subscribe in order to join a Community Church, or a set of beliefs to which a Community Church must subsribe in order to join the Council.[15]

A Community Church from this particular council does not have a set of biblical and theological beliefs, a creed to which an individual must subscribe in order to be a church member. But what about the belief that Jesus is the way, the truth, and the life, and that no one can come to the Father but through Him? Any belief that is dogmatic must be dropped for the sake of unity.

> This is a Community Church as I conceive it ought to be: a church organized democratically, free from the domination of dogma, money, and sectarianism, aiming to decrease the number of sects by the process of absorption and welding.[16]

Are you running enthusiastically toward ecumenical unity?

---

[14]Ralph Shotwell, *Unity Without Uniformity* (Community Church Press, 1984), p. 41.
[15]Ralph Shotwell, ibid., p. 42.
[16]Ralph Shotwell, ibid., p. 39.

Is there a limit on what will be compromised for that unity? There is a true ecumenical unity among those who have placed their faith in Christ's substitutionary death on the cross. But the basis for true unity can be denied for the sake of unity with cults and other religions.

A spokesman for a large denomination once said concerning cults that their theology, their exploitation of the susceptable, or even their manipulative tactics were not a concern for him as long as the people involved were having their needs met and were happy. Is this the message of Christ?

Conclusion

There is a dynamic in doctrine, like an intricate spider web. When you touch one edge of the web, the effect ripples across the rest of the web. The deviations of the doctrine of salvation can be diagnosed by their relationship to Jesus, who they say He was, and what they say He accomplished upon the cross.

Jesus was God and able to live well enough to be a perfect sacrifice. He died on the cross as our substitute and finished the work of salvation completely. A mutant doctrine of salvation would say that either Jesus did not complete His work on the cross and we are responsible to help earn it, or some other individual should be the object of our faith, or there really was no need for Jesus to die because sin is no real problem.

A final problem with a mutant doctrine of salvation is that, just as most mutants, it is sterile. It cannot produce what it was created for. It cannot save.

◆ 10 ◆

Faith That Works

While good works are not able to save an individual, they are evidence of true faith. Before works can truly please God, they must come from a regenerated heart. It is like washing dishes with greasy hands. If I work on my car, then attempt to help my wife wash the dishes, I may do all the right things, but because my hands are greasy, the dishes come out dirty no matter how well or how hard I work. Similarly, worshiping in church with sin in one's heart, though all appears proper, means little to God. The righteous acts of Pharisees with unclean hearts angered Jesus.

But if the grease and oil were first washed from my hands, the dishes would come out clean. It is not that the technique was changed, or that the intensity was shifted, but because the hands were first cleaned. Evidence of clean hands is clean dishes. Evidence of a clean heart is good works.

When all you see is the result of salvation, you might incorrectly assume that the evidence of grace is the means to grace, that good works are the basis of salvation. The external expression does not save, the inner faith does.

What is the relationship between the inner faith and the outward good works? As we have seen, Paul certainly sees that man is justified by faith apart from works, and that works are a result of a new nature.

However, there are a number of scripture passages in which the primary purpose is not to define that relationship, but to address other issues. Unfortunately, some of those texts appear to imply the necessity of works to be saved. Cults often appeal to those texts to substantiate the need for works, even though this is not the primary purpose of these texts. In this chapter we will respond to some of these scriptures.

Keep the Commandments

It is often asked, "If we are saved by grace and not works, why does the Bible teach that we are to keep the commandments?"

The only point we will mention is that even in the Old Testament, the saints were saved solely by faith. Their obedience to the law demonstrated that faith. In fact, Jesus' conflict with the Pharisees was that they expected to gain salvation by fulfilling the letter of the law, by traditions-legalism.

The admonitions to keep the commandments can be viewed in various ways. One way is found in Matt. 19:16–17 and points to the need of salvation through Christ.

> Now a man came up to Jesus and asked, "Teacher, what good thing must I do to get eternal life?" "Why do you ask me about what is good?" Jesus replied. "There is only One who is good. If you want to enter life, obey the commandments."

A rich young ruler approaches Jesus asking Him how he might obtain eternal life. Jesus responds that he should keep the commandments. He recognizes that this young man feels self-righteous and self-justified, so Jesus attempts to show that only God is righteous. The young man responds by asking, "Which ones?" In other words, "What's a passing score?" He feels that he is just and righteous from the list Jesus has provided. Jesus asks the young man to sell his possessions. This demonstrated that the young man had failed in keeping the very first of the Ten Commandments, "You shall have no other gods before me" (Deut. 5:7). When Jesus asks this question, He prefaces it with, "If you want to be perfect . . ." (v. 21).

If we wish to earn our salvation, we must be perfect. We have already established this. The disciples recognized the difficulty of this and asked, "Who then can be saved?" (v. 25). Certainly, if the rich with all their wealth and influence could not earn salvation, then who could? Jesus responded, "With men this is impossible, but with God all things are possible." How is it possible with God? Through Jesus Christ. In this passage Jesus is not advocating works salvation but the need for grace.

A second text which deals with the keeping of commandments is John 14:15: "If you love me, you will obey what I command." Is Jesus saying that to be saved, we must keep the law? Is He saying that to *keep* our salvation, we must continue to keep the law? The answer is, "No." It is not the Old Testament law to which Jesus refers, but to "His" commandments. He has made clear that loving one another encompasses these (John 13:34; 15:12).

The issue is not, "If you do not keep the commandments, you will not be saved," but, "If you love me, then that love will be demonstrated in obedience." This idea is also consistent with the gospel.

John also wrote in his first epistle about the need to live a holy life. He concluded chapter 3 by saying:

> Those who obey his commands live in him, and he in them. And this is how we know that he lives in us: We know it by the Spirit he gave us. (1 John 3:24)

Is John advocating salvation by works? Read the preceding verse.

> And this is his command: to believe in the name of his Son Jesus Christ, and to love one another, as he commanded us. (1 John 3:23)

Be Perfect

If salvation is by grace and not dependent upon works, then why does Jesus teach us to be perfect?

> Be perfect, therefore, as your heavenly Father is perfect. (Matt. 5:48)

The word "perfect" (*teleioi*) can also be translated "complete" or "mature." In this context, Jesus condemns the practice of loving our neighbors but hating our enemies. In other words, the Jews were showing partiality. Jesus said they should love everyone.

Since their heavenly Father loves perfectly, they, too, were expected to love the Gentiles and not be partial. Salvation through perfection is not the issue here.

Because God is holy and perfect, we as His children should strive to reflect that holiness. We will stumble. John has said that anyone who claims that he does not stumble, but is perfect, is a liar (1 John 1:8–10). However, the Scriptures still demand that we strive for that goal and not give up. Paul recognized that he himself, even as an apostle, was not perfect (Phil. 3:12–13). He advocated that we forget what lies behind, and reach forward to the goal. The perfect, or mature, will strive for this goal. Several scriptures give testimony that personal perfection is that goal: Eph. 4:13; James 1:4; 2 Cor. 13:9–11.

In spite of the fact that we have not done everything perfectly, we are seen as perfect in the eyes of God because we have been justified through Jesus Christ.

> Because by one sacrifice he has made perfect forever those who are being made holy. (Heb. 10:14)

Ultimately, the Christian will be perfected, not through his own efforts, but by God himself.

> Being confident of this, that he who began a good work in you will [perfect it, NASV] carry it on to completion until the day of Christ Jesus. (Phil. 1:6)

> And the God of all grace, who called you to his eternal glory in Christ, after you have suffered a little while, will himself [perfect, NASV] restore you and make you strong, firm and steadfast. (1 Pet. 5:10)

Work Out Your Salvation

When Paul was writing to the Philippians, both he and they were experiencing problems. He was in jail. They were having problems with lack of harmony in the church. In this context Paul challenged them:

> Therefore, my dear friends, as you have always obeyed—not only in my presence, but now much more in my absence—continue to work out your salvation with fear and trembling. (Phil. 2:12)

Was he teaching that they were to earn their salvation? No. He already stated that God began a good work in them and that

God would finish it (Phil. 1:6). In this context, Paul does not say "work *for* your salvation," but "work *out* your salvation," because God was working *in* them (v. 13).

Paul's point was simple: since God is working in you, you work out, or reflect your salvation. Specifically speaking, find a solution to the internal quarrels. Be obedient, even when I'm not around. If God is working in you, you should respond obediently and find a solution.

A Final Judgment Based Upon Works

> All the nations will be gathered before him, and he will separate the people one from another as a shepherd separates the sheep from the goats. He will put the sheep on his right and the goats on his left. Then the King will say to those on his right, "Come, you who are blessed by my Father; take your inheritance, the kingdom prepared for you since the creation of the world. For I was hungry and you gave me something to eat, I was thirsty and you gave me something to drink, I was a stranger and you invited me in, I needed clothes and you clothed me, I was sick and you looked after me, I was in prison and you came to visit me." (Matt. 25:32–36)

The scene is the judgment seat, and Jesus is judging the nations. Sheep and goats will be separated. Those who have done good deeds will inherit the kingdom of God, and those who did not will be sent into eternal fire. If God is using works as criteria, then aren't works the basis for salvation?

It is very interesting that those who are allowed to enter the kingdom of God seem confused that they are entering because they ministered to Jesus by ministering to those in need. Clearly, it was not their intent to do good deeds to earn salvation, but they did good deeds for compassionate reasons. It seemed to be natural for them. On the other hand, those who were not allowed to enter the kingdom of God were confused also. They did not feed "Jesus" when He was hungry, clothe Him, etc. Apparently, their attitude was, "If I'd known it was you, I would have done it." What it revealed was their selfish motivation and evil nature.

If we were to conclude that this teaches works salvation, then we have conflicting signals coming to us from Jesus. Matt. 7:21–

23 says that even people who do many good deeds in Jesus' name will be excluded from the kingdom. In John 8:24 Jesus said, "If you do not believe that I am the one I claim to be, you will indeed die in your sins." These verses are just two examples where Jesus taught that faith in himself was the key to entering the kingdom of God.

Recall that Matthew is a gospel written primarily to those of a Jewish background. It is rich in Jewish traditions, practices, and nuances.

A strong theme in Jewish tradition is the judgment of God. God is the judge who judges righteously. Only the righteous shall enter the kingdom of God. Those entering the kingdom are righteous because their hearts apparently bear righteous fruit. How did their hearts become righteous when all mankind was sinful? How could they possess a nature which produced good works?

The New Testament shows us the way to righteousness. When we place our faith in Jesus Christ, we are justified (Rom. 5:1). We became a new creation (2 Cor. 5:17). "We were by nature objects of wrath," but Jesus "made us alive" (Eph. 2:3, 5).

We are no longer under condemnation (Rom. 8:1). However, when God separates the righteous from the unrighteous, the Christian will have true proof of Jesus' redemption and righteousness: the good fruit of good deeds. This will prove that we are truly righteous. It is not that Christians will be doing good works to earn their salvation, but that God will be able to point to our works as proof that we are righteous. Remember, the sheep were confused about their having met Jesus' needs. What they did was the natural result of being in Christ and possessing a new nature. The ability to be truly righteous comes from God, not from our sinful flesh.

James, Chapter Two

The most difficult text to evaluate in the works/grace debate is found in James, chapter two. This section is difficult to understand because it includes terms such as "justify," "works," "salvation," and "law," which Paul used in the previous scriptures, but now James seems to be making the opposite conclusion. Certainly Paul was addressing the issue of the relationship of works and salvation as his primary intent. The other passages which we discussed appeared to contradict those conclusions, had different primary purposes. But it appears here that James has the primary purpose of explaining the works/grace issue.

The second chapter of James is one of the *most frequently cited texts by cultists*. Notice some portions taken from James, chapter two, NASV:

> Was not Abraham our father justified by works, when he offered up Isaac his son on the altar? (v 21)

> You see that faith was working with his works, and as a result of the works, faith was perfected; (v. 22)

> And the Scripture was fulfilled which says, "And Abraham believed God, and it was reckoned to him as righteousness," and he was called the friend of God. (v. 23)

> You see that a man is justified by works, and not by faith alone. (v. 24)

> For just as the body without the spirit is dead, so also faith without works is dead. (v. 26)

Scripture is God's Word and, therefore, is consistent and noncontradictory. Yet, the appearance is that James and Paul are having a disagreement over the relationship of works and salvation. As believers, it is our responsibility to find harmony between these two inspired authors. As we follow some basic rules of interpretation, we can resolve this difficulty.

Paul and James were addressing different audiences with different problems and with different purposes. The relationship of faith and works by each author must be examined with an understanding of the limitations of these entirely different contexts.

The Roman audience Paul was addressing in the Book of Romans was apparently experiencing some conflict over undue emphasis on Jewish tradition and law. The epistle to the Galatians is addressed clearly to Gentiles who are being persuaded to follow Jewish law. The purpose for these writings was very specific: to correct the false perspective that Gentiles must fulfill certain works of the law to earn salvation. Paul was not against the law.

He said that it was good (Rom. 7:7, 12). He recognized that it revealed the righteousness of God and defined which actions were unholy and sinful. Paul's argument was that we are unable to earn our salvation by doing works of the law. Good works are a result of true faith.

On the other hand, James was writing to Jewish Christians. By this time there had been an overreaction to the gospel of grace that Paul had worked so earnestly to teach them. The pendulum had swung to the side of antinomianism. The term *antinomianism* is derived from two Greek words: *anti* (against), and *nomos* (law). It means to totally reject the moral law. A more modern term is *license*.

Some early Christians were abusing grace and not living lives that were characterized by freedom from the law of sin and death. The purpose of James was to motivate the people to conduct themselves properly, to be conformed to the righteousness of God. They knew the Word but did not follow it (James 1:22, 23; 2:1, 4, 8, 15, 16). They talked of religion, but did not live it.

There are four words that play a major role in James: *religion*, *faith*, *works*, and *justify*. It is quite common in evangelical Christianity to insist that Christianity is not a religion, but a relationship. Certainly this contrast is valid. However, James does not compare "religion" to "relationship," but true religion with false religion. His emphasis is on the character of religion. True religion produces good fruit. False religion is all talk and no action, all show and no go. To James, true religion is the practice of one's faith.

"Faith" is a second word of importance in this chapter, used in contrasting true religion to false religion. In those clauses describing false religion, faith is modified by *dead, barren, without works*. On the other hand, the faith describing true religion is confirmed *by works*.

The third word is "works." Part of the problem with "works" is its relationship to the Mosaic law, the Jewish ceremonial law. Sometimes "works" is used in relationship to the law, especially by Paul when he demonstrates that these kinds of works are insufficient to justify the individual. Paul was emphatic when he said that "no one will be declared righteous in his sight by observing the law" (Rom. 3:20).

The question is: Does "works" always refer to a means of salvation or can it mean something else? The answer is that context determines the meaning of a word. The Greek word for works, *ergon*, has been used in a variety of ways in a variety of contexts. But generally, *ergon* means "actions" or "deeds" and is neutral. The kind of actions are described by the modifiers in the context.

Paul and James are using *ergon* in different ways. *Ergon* in James means "actions" or "deeds." The most authoritative Greek lexicon by Bauer, Arndt, and Gingrich, confirms this definition in relationship to James 2:8–12.[1]

In his situation, James is saying that good actions are the evidence of true faith. This idea is confirmed by Colin Brown's *Dictionary of New Testament Theology*:

> As a designation of the actions of the believer, *ergon* can be used synonymously with *karpos*—fruit.[2]

Fruit is the visible evidence of the inner nature. The fruit (*karpos*) of the Spirit (Gal. 5:22) is the evidence of God's Spirit within the believer. In the same chapter, the flesh is characterized by works (*ergon*) of the flesh. It is important to see that in James 2:18, the verb "show" is used in relationship to faith and works, emphasizing the visible, external proof of inner faith. This proof is also mentioned by Titus 1:16.

> They claim to know God, but by their actions [*ergon*] they deny him. They are detestable, disobedient and unfit for anything good [*ergon*].

Probably the most crucial word is "justify." *Dikaioo* is the Greek verb generally translated "justify." It is based upon the same Greek root word as "righteous" (*dikaios*). That is why "dikaioo" is sometimes translated as "make righteous." Justification in reference to God is a legal term. When God as a judge pronounced a person righteous, the righteousness is imputed, not earned. Paul, addressing a Gentile audience, and attempting to

---

[1]Walter Bauer, William F. Arndt, and F. Wilbur Gingrich, *A Greek-English Lexicon of the New Testament and Other Early Christian Literature* (Chicago: The University of Chicago Press, 1957), p. 307.

[2]Colin Brown, *The New International Dictionary of New Testament Theology* (Grand Rapids, Mich.: Zondervan Publishing House, 1975), vol. 3, p. 1149.

emphasize this judicial decree, focused upon the completed and confirmed standing an individual has in Christ (Rom. 5:1).

> Therefore, since we have been justified through faith, we have peace with God through our Lord Jesus Christ.

However, James is writing to a Jewish audience. According to Jewish rabbinic tradition, vindication is a key ingredient of justification. The emphasis is not on the fact, but on the vindication, or confirmation, of that fact. James emphasizes evidence: works.

Both Paul and James refer to God's justification, but Paul emphasizes the legal standing based upon faith, not works. James emphasizes that justification on a spiritual level is confirmed by actions.

In James 2:21, James uses Abraham as an example. James precedes this example by saying that faith without works is barren. The lead-in is obvious. One of the reasons Abraham needed faith was that God had promised to multiply Abraham's seed while his wife was elderly and "barren." His faith was honored by his son Isaac, the fruit of Abraham's faith.

Paul also uses Abraham as an example of faith in Romans, chapter 4. The issue is whether Abraham was justified by works (the ritual of circumcision) or by faith. The promise to Abraham was fulfilled neither by circumcision nor by the law, but by faith (4:9–19).

Similarly, in Gal. 3:6–13, Paul again refers to Abraham as an illustration of justification by faith. His point is clear. The promise was to be received by the Gentiles by faith, apart from works of the law.

Conclusion

The importance of this chapter can be seen in several ways. First of all, when evangelizing those in the cults, our goal is their salvation. But in order for a cultist to put his complete trust in Christ for salvation, he must understand the completed work of Christ on the cross, and acknowledge that this is the teaching of Scripture. Some of the verses that I discussed in this chapter are barriers to that aknowledgment. Once those barriers have been eliminated, the gospel can have a great effect upon the cultist's life.

Some prefer a works salvation gospel because grace is so foreign to much of our culture, and because, as we have stated before, the flesh desires to claim part of the glory for salvation. Even so, the gospel is the liberating message from the tyranny of having to do good works. The gospel is the Good News because only the assurance of Christ's work on the cross lifts the burden of redemption off us.

Many cultists would love to be freed if they felt that salvation by grace were truly biblical. Once I was disicipling a family that had left the Mormon church and become Christians. As we talked, one theme kept resurfacing; their Mormon friends were very discouraged that they would never reach *exultation*, the stage of afterlife where the faithful Mormon becomes a god. But the Bible says that our place before God is guaranteed only because Jesus has been exalted; because He died, rose, and ascended to heaven to prepare us a place there with Him.

A second application of this chapter is our awareness of how Bible verses can be used to shift away from the gospel of grace in Christianity. On one occasion, I opened my pulpit to an official representative of a large, independent mission agency that our church had supported for several years. As he began to speak, I began to feel very uncomfortable. He discussed the meaning of the gospel and poked fun at Christians who believed in being "born again" and "saved" at one moment in time (a group which included me).

He continued his ridicule by saying that no one is saved by a simple act of faith, but that salvation is a lifetime process. When salvation is considered a process like this, then grace has shifted to a works mentality.

Study Questions for Part III

1. What must we do to earn salvation by our own merits?
2. Are we able to earn salvation by our own works?
3. What is Jesus' part in salvation?
4. What was Jesus' relationship to the law?
5. What is the plan of salvation?
6. What did Jesus accomplish on the cross?
7. What is the relationship of works to salvation?
8. How do cults alter the plan of salvation?
9. What do some cults teach about works?
10. How do some cults alter the object of faith in salvation?
11. What do some cults teach about the existence of sin?
12. How do some cults challenge biblically the plan of salvation?
13. How do some cults distort passages on keeping the commandments?
14. How do some cults distort passages about being perfect?
15. How do some cults distort James 2 to establish works salvation?

PART IV

The Bible

Striking Bedrock: The Basis of Truth

Rumors are usually just grown-up lies. But as the reports came in from Jonestown, Guyana, rumors proved true. What we thought were exaggerations turned horribly factual: murder squads, the slaughter of news reporters, the assassination of a U.S. Congressman, and the mass suicide of over 900 people.

Not only did this tragedy spark interest in cults, it also produced a considerable number of questions. Is the People's Temple unique? How could 900 people be motivated to commit suicide? Were the people brainwashed? Why would rational adults set aside firm values to do things clearly against the moral norms of their culture and religious upbringing? The answers to these questions are found in the subject of authority.

Authority is the basis by which we live our lives. Our decisions, our values, and our conduct are all rooted in some form of authority. It could be our parents, peers, an institution, a legal code, ourselves, or a hero. No one lives without some sort of authority.

The Search for Authority

Although man has always been self-centered, he has generally acknowledged some external authority. But authority has been gradually shifting away from government and religion to the individual. Values, decisions, and conduct are being based on what pleases me. We like to take care of Number One. As self-elevating philosophies have grown, people have often pitted their will against authority. We often hear phrases like, "No one has the right to tell *me* what to do," and, "My body is my own property; I'll do what *I* want."

This shift in the nature of authority has had an affect on cults in America. Those attempting to resurrect the "benevolent purposes" of the sixties have found fulfillment in some of the cults. Others, having jumped with both feet into self-gratification, have found a haven in one of the many Eastern existential cults. There they "find themselves" and discover "God consciousness" also.

Other seekers, fearful and insecure, are looking for an authority to make their decisions for them, to turn off their minds, to relieve them of conflict. The fastest growing religious groups are often those that legalistically lift the decision-making process from the frustrated seeker. Many desire some form of religious experience. Disappointed with traditional American religion, they are joining new religious organizations characterized by warmth and life. Some find true Christian fellowships; some do not.

Many seek a strong authority. Others, rejecting any external authority, bounce from one cult to another, submitting only as long as their needs are met.

We all seek a reason for living, some basis of authority. But the ultimate question we need to ask is, Is our authority credible? In the present age, with its emphasis on self-rule, there is no greater evidence than Jonestown, Guyana, of the fact that it does matter what you believe.

The Bible: Bedrock Truth

The Christian recognizes that there is a greater authority than himself: God. God does not promote selfishness and rebellion, but submission and repentance. What we know about God is what He chose to reveal to us in the Scriptures. There He has revealed His character and will. This revelation becomes our authority for living as Christians because it reveals the God we worship.

We can have confidence in Scripture because of its credibility. It is trustworthy. Except for a small percent of manuscript discrepancies that have been clearly defined and dealt with, we know we have almost exactly what the original authors wrote. In reference to the New Testament, the popular misconception that today's translations are based on other translations is inaccurate. Our English Bibles are accurate translations of God's revelation.

Eyewitness Accounts

The question of reliability stands on the credibility of the authors. Were they trustworthy? Or did they intend to deceive us? Historically, their integrity stands.

For example, the New Testament apostles wrote of being eye-witnesses to miraculous events. The Apostle John in his first epistle (1:1–3) appeals to readers as an eyewitness.

The Apostle Peter also speaks from his personal experience:

> We did not follow cleverly invented stories when we told you about the power and coming of our Lord Jesus Christ, but we were eyewitnesses of his majesty. (2 Pet. 1:16)

Paul, who was not one of the twelve disciples, also claims to be one of the many eyewitnesses of the resurrected Christ.

> For what I received I passed on to you as of first importance: that Christ died for our sins according to the Scriptures, that he was buried, that he was raised on the third day according to the Scriptures, and that he appeared to Peter, and then to the Twelve. After that, he appeared to more than five hundred of the brothers at the same time, most of whom are still living, though some have fallen asleep. Then he appeared to James, then to all the apostles, and last of all he appeared to me also, as to one abnormally born. (1 Cor. 15:3–8)

Luke, although not an apostle, claims to be writing on the basis of eyewitness testimony.

> Many have undertaken to draw up an account of the things that have been fulfilled among us, just as they were handed down to us by those who from the first were eyewitnesses and servants of the word. Therefore, since I myself have carefully investigated everything from the beginning, it seemed good also to me to write an orderly account for you, most excellent Theophilus, so that you may know the certainty of the things you have been taught. (Luke 1:1–4)

The men who testified of seeing Jesus after His resurrection were aware of the implications of their statements. A resurrec-

tion is hardly an everyday occurrence. If there had been no resurrection, these men who claimed to be eyewitnesses would have
had to conspire to propagate the story. Yet, at different times
and different places, each of these men was willing to die for his
testimony (only John died a natural death). Would these men
have willingly died for a lie they had conspired to promote? It
would have accomplished nothing. Therefore, we can be sure
that the text is reliable and the authors are credible![1]

God-Breathed Revelation

These authors chose to give Scripture considerable authority,
treating it as a document inspired by God. Paul emphasized the
importance of Scripture and its source.

> All Scripture is God-breathed and is useful for teaching, rebuk-
> ing, correcting and training in righteousness. (2 Tim. 3:16)

The most important aspect of this text is that "all Scripture
is God-breathed." Even though Paul is referring to the Old Testament, he states that a characteristic of Scripture is that it is *God-
breathed*. Consequently, if in the time of the early church more
writings had been considered Scripture, then they would also
carry the same God-breathed characteristic. This seems to be the
view of the New Testament authors.

For example, when Peter was speaking of that which was to
come, he made a reference to Paul's writings. Peter stated that
people distort Paul's words as they do with all of Paul's letters.
Peter placed great authority on *all* of Paul's writings, or he would
not have pronounced such severe consequence for distorting
Paul's words. Even more significant is the fact that Peter equates
Paul's writings with the rest of Scripture.

> Bear in mind that our Lord's patience means salvation, just as
> our dear brother Paul also wrote you with the wisdom that God
> gave him. He writes the same way in all his letters, speaking in
> them of these matters. His letters contain some things that are
> hard to understand, which ignorant and unstable people distort,
> as they do the other Scriptures, to their own destruction. (2 Pet.
> 3:15–16)

---

[1]For more information on this subject, see F.F. Bruce, *New Testament Documents:
Are They Reliable?* (Downers Grove, Ill.: InterVarsity Press).

Because Scripture is God-breathed, it stimulates spiritual growth when properly understood and obediently followed (1 Pet. 2:2). As a result, we are commanded to be students of its contents, able to properly understand it (2 Tim. 2:15). The Bible is the basis for Christian faith and practice: our authority. In the previous parts of this book we looked at Christ, the nature of God, and the means of salvation. Distorting truths concerning these results in separation from God. The Scripture is clear on that. Even so, history has demonstrated that when one denies the authority of God's Word, then in time, those crucial doctrines are always distorted, bringing serious consequences (2 Pet. 3:16). Once Scripture is devalued, the natural, logical conclusion is the denial of its teachings and the concession of important doctrinal truths.

One of the distinctive characteristics of cults is the altering of the Bible's authority. How else could one justify many clearly unbiblical perspectives and practices?

Cults and Biblical Authority

There are a vast number of cults. Some hold tenaciously to the Bible as God's Word, some do not. Although cults may vary as to how they view the Bible, all will alter it as the sole source of theological authority. This is one of the indications that a group has moved from orthodoxy and may be cultic.

One category of cults denies the authority of the Bible entirely. Recognizing the uncomfortable posture their creeds have with the Scriptures, they choose not to harmonize their views but simply to dismiss the source of conflict: Scripture. They say things like, "The Bible is not a good authority because . . . it is full of errors, it has been altered by Satan, it is not as complete, it is out-dated, or it needs to be interpreted by the . . ."

There are several other explanations usually given by cults holding to the Bible as God's Word yet ignoring its authority. "The Bible is our authority, *plus* these other inspired writings." The cultists will contend that other writings are either equal with the Bible, greater than the Bible, or explain the Bible more clearly.

The Bible is our authority as long as it is translated correctly. One must admit that there are a number of translations of the Bible. But many cult translations have unjustified additions, deletions, or alterations. Usually those texts that are harmful to their positions are modified without grammatical or lexical basis.

The Bible is our authority, but only as our prophet interprets it. This view claims biblical authority, but in reality, it favors an individual, personal authority. Ambiguous, difficult, or contradictory passages that deny the teachings of the cult are easily "cleared up" by the new revelation of an enlightened individual. Of great significance is that this prophet is not limited by the actual words or grammar of the text, but is able to see between the lines to what is not really there, to what is indiscernible by others' eyes.

Sometimes entire groups of adherents claim a special insight that orthodox Christians lack. The practical result is that the Bible really loses its authority. After I had had a hearty discussion on a doctrinal issue with a cultist, the leader responded, "You may be right on a purely grammatical level, but if you had the Spirit as we have, you would not even question our interpretation. Only the spiritually intune are able to understand the meaning." This implies that the Bible is not understandable on its own merits, but that it can be twisted in any way they desire without regard to what the inspired author meant.

Another view alters biblical authority by totally replacing it with personal authority or a personal occult experience. *We each have direct experiential knowledge of God. We do not learn ideas, we experience. We don't do, we feel. We don't learn about God from the visible, we are in direct contact with Him.*

This elevating of experience over biblical revelation as the final measure of truth has been working its way into the church. All too often we hear accusations that some Christians understand the Bible only on an intellectual level. Unfortunately, it is the person who knows Christ personally who is accused of being too logical. He is told, "You must let God speak to your heart directly about this matter."

But how does God do that? Some Christians today are advocating that there must be an internal confirmation, some existential feeling. How is this different from the neo-orthodox theologian who states that the Bible *becomes* the Word of God as he is emotionally moved? How does this differ from the cult leader who appeals to his own special knowledge? Has some deep emotional spiritual experience replaced the Bible as our final authority?

God would not reveal anything different to your heart than what He has said in His Bible. If we believe the Bible is inerrant, we must allow it the authority we claim that it has.

Christians who elevate experience sometimes attempt to "pull rank" and defend their views by the statement, "God spoke to my heart and told me . . ." Whatever God happened to tell this person usually agrees with their position. They take security in the fact that you may argue about the grammar of the text, but you cannot argue about their experience.

An example of this may be seen in one response to Dave Hunt's *The Seduction of Christianity.* One man felt that he had not been properly quoted, so he responded to the book on the basis of three prophecies which he had received from God.

His second prophecy dealt with a delusion he felt was sweeping Christianity.

> Subsequently I prophesied that another wave of delusion would sweep the country, this one claiming righteousness but insidious and destructive, creating great division within the Body. That turned out to be one of the fruits of *The Seduction of Christianity.*[2]

He goes on to state in his third prophecy:

> The Lord's actual words to me were: "Great divisiveness is coming in the Body. It will be worse than that caused by Hunt. Men will seek righteousness and find it by trumpeting various causes, instead of in My blood. They shall therefore seek the blood of others and exalt themselves as the righteous ones. The entire movement of holiness shall turn to Phariseeism, for My people have not sought the heart's righteousness and therefore will seek to find it in exterior observances. The Pharisees arise in every generation, My children. It is they who persecute Me in every age. Warn the Body in your next newsletter."[3]

This man indicts Hunt by claiming to prophesy for God. And

---

[2]John Sanford, "A Word from John Sanford," *Mission Messsenger,* July-August 1986, p. 7.
[3]John Sanford, ibid.

if he means these are "the Lord's actual words," then they are inerrant. If they are, then Hunt is terribly wrong. But, while I did not agree with everything that Dave Hunt wrote, he hit the nail right on the head in many cases.

I cannot say for sure that God did not give these three prophecies. That is the security of standing upon untestable experience. But I feel particularly uncomfortable with the nuance of the last one. Time will tell its source, but the principle remains true: we must be very careful in the church before we speak for God.

When we begin to speak flippantly about how "God told me this," we need to be clear of the implications of what we are saying. If it is only an *impression* or a *feeling* that we think God has given us, then we need to be sure that flavor comes across. If we believe that God has audibly spoken to us—and I won't limit God's ability to do so—we have a special responsibility to get the counsel and advice of respected Christian men.

While working with college students, I encountered a hardworking Christian who was very active in the faith. As it turned out, he claimed that God spoke to him audibly. In time, those conversations became more complicated; not only did God the Father speak but also God the Son, and God the Holy Spirit. After a while, the voices of the Trinity began disagreeing with one another and arguing. So much for being of God.

When God spoke to people in the Bible, there was always a special purpose for it. All too frequently today, people are cocking their heads slightly, pausing, and responding to God's verbal cues on a regular basis about some unimportant issue. Some cultist may turn to us and say, "So what's the difference between what you're doing and what I am doing?" In all honesty, we may have to admit, "Nothing."

Testing for False Prophets

The Bible refers to several prophets. Many cult leaders claim to be prophets of similar degree. But if they are prophets of God, do they not have the authority to interpret Scripture and give new revelation? The question is: *How can one tell if a prophet is true or false?* The Bible gives three criteria for judging a prophet.

First, if he predicts the future, 100 percent of his prophecy must come true.

> "But a prophet who presumes to speak in my name anything I have not commanded him to say, or a prophet who speaks in the name of other gods, must be put to death." You may say to yourselves, "How can we know when a message has not been spoken by the LORD?" If what a prophet proclaims in the name of the Lord does not take place or come true, that is a message the Lord has not spoken. That prophet has spoken presumptuously. Do not be afraid of him. (Deut. 18:20–22)

The prophecies of many leaders shed doubt on their call from God.

The second is that the prophet leads people toward serving God. Does he lead men to serve the biblical God, or away from God and toward himself?

> If a prophet, or one who foretells by dreams, appears among you and announces to you a miraculous sign or wonder, and if the sign or wonder of which he has spoken takes place, and he says, "Let us follow other gods" (gods you have not known) "and let us worship them," you must not listen to the words of that prophet or dreamer. The Lord your God is testing you to find out whether you love him with all your heart and with all your soul. (Deut. 13:1–3)

Third, compare his revelation with biblical revelation. Does it agree? Or contradict? Are his methods and values consistent with Scripture? Does his interpretation of Scripture agree with the clear meaning? Scripture is not to be toyed with; it is the Holy Spirit's property:

> Above all, you must understand that no prophecy of Scripture came about by the prophet's own interpretation. For prophecy never had its origin in the will of man, but men spoke from God as they were carried along by the Holy Spirit. (2 Pet. 1:20–21)

The Bible also instructs us to be wary of false prophets. It teaches us to test the spirits to see if they are from God:

> Dear friends, do not believe every spirit, but test the spirits to see whether they are from God, because many false prophets have gone out into the world. (1 John 4:1)

The Bible teaches us to examine prophecy:

> Do not put out the Spirit's fire, do not treat prophecies with contempt. Test everything. Hold on to the good. (1 Thess. 5:19–21)

The Bereans in Acts 17:11 were called more noble because they checked out the words of the teachers to see if they conformed to previous revealed truth.

> Now the Bereans were of more noble character than the Thessalonians, for they received the message with great eagerness and examined the Scriptures every day to see if what Paul said was true.

Cults and Authority

All cults will, in one way or another, alter biblical authority. Some use one of the previously mentioned ways, some use several different ways. The Mormon church exemplifies three of those methods. They claim to have a living prophet whose authority is passed on. They use several scriptures besides the Bible: the *Book of Mormon, Doctrine and Covenants,* and *The Pearl of Great Price.* Joseph Smith also wrote his own translation of the Bible.

This is principally the method of the Jehovah's Witnesses. They have created a new Bible called *The New World Translation of the Holy Scriptures.* Even more, their leaders often speak with prophetic authority. Walter Martin, author of *The Kingdom of the Cults,* describes it this way:

> No less an example of this was Charles Taze Russell's bold claim that his writings were indispensable to the study of the Bible for the Jehovah's Witnesses, and that to study the Bible apart from his inspired comments was to go into spiritual darkness. Russell also taught that concentration upon his writings even at the expense of studying the Bible would certainly lead one into deeper spiritual illumination within five years.[4]

Christian Science also has a prophetess, named Mary Baker Eddy, and her extra-biblical scripture entitled *Science and Health with Key to the Scriptures.* An interesting necessity for Christian

---

[4]Walter Martin, *The Kingdom of the Cults* (Minneapolis, Minn.: Bethany House Publishers, 1965), p. 26.

Science is that it also must deny the accuracy of the Bible. Mary Baker Eddy wrote:

> The decisions by vote of Church Councils as to what should and should not be considered Holy Writ; the manifest mistakes in ancient versions; the thirty thousand different readings in the Old Testament, and the three hundred thousand in the New— these facts show how a mortal and material sense stole into the divine record, with its own hue darkening to some extent the inspired pages.[5]

Armstrong's Worldwide Church of God tenaciously holds to the Bible as God's Word, and continuously advocates that all people should "read it for themselves" to see that Armstrong is speaking the truth. But Armstrong is not hesitant to say that the orthodox faith interprets the Bible differently. This does not bother him. He resolves all conflicts from his own prophetic revelation.

> Let's choose to be biblical rather than "orthodox" and see what is the reward of the saved as revealed in the Scriptures.[6]

> I wonder if you realize that every Truth of GOD, accepted as true DOCTRINE and BELIEF in the World-wide Church of God, came from Christ through me, or was finally approved and made official through me.[7]

In some cases a group may claim that its leaders are only interpreting the Bible, and that the Bible is their sole authority. However, a good test to make is to watch what they do when their leaders' interpretations clearly contradict Scripture. Do they adhere to the interpretation or the Bible? This may reveal their true authority.

The followers of William Marrion Branham also have a prophet, now deceased, who has left other writings that claim special authority. One of his followers tells us:

> These tapes are records of visions and experiences that bring "thus saith the Lord," to the Bride. He said we were to hear the

---

[5]Mary Baker Eddy, *Science and Health with Key to the Scriptures* (Boston, Mass.: The First Church of Christ, Scientist, 1971), p. 139.
[6]Jon Hill, "A Tale of Two Prophets," Part 6, *The Plain Truth*, July 1977, p. 20.
[7]Herbert W. Armstrong, "Personal from Herbert W. Armstrong: How I Came to Be Going to Kings and Heads of Government," *The Plain Truth*, Feb. 1977, p. 17.

tapes. He said that they were the Message. Yet the question arises, as to how a man could be so presumptuous as to believe that what he said was the Word of God. The answer is, the same way Paul could be sure. . . .[8]

To me, the Message is spiritual authority; yet I had difficulty thinking of it as Scripture, because it wasn't written in script. But I have no hesitancy whatsoever for saying it is "thus saith the Lord." Therefore I say it is the Word of God.[9]

Meanwhile, many Eastern cults simply deny the uniqueness of the Bible saying that it is equal to other religious writings. All these writings are vehicles that aid their devotees in contacting and experiencing god.

The Bible and the Cults

Why do people with Christian backgrounds join cults? Our emphasis is a doctrinal, not a sociological, evaluation of cults. However, the Bible as an authority and sociological characteristics of cults do agree on this issue.

Many are ignorant of biblical truth. They are easily deceived into thinking that cults are legitimate, orthodox denominations. Some cults mislead people by withholding the complete truth until they have a firm hold on the convert. They start with common areas of agreement and then slowly show their true allegiance and what they believe. This is why so many groups who do not believe that the Bible is God's Word use it so frequently. They understand that the Bible is respected as a religious authority in our culture. They can quote scripture to appeal to religious individuals.

They lead individuals over a bridge toward the cult. The bridge is the common ground of agreement, often the Bible. After the disciple has crossed the bridge, authority is transferred to something or someone, and then constantly reinforced. When the bridge is finally destroyed, there is no easy way back.

---

[8]Pearry Green, *The Acts of the Prophet* (Tucson, Ariz.: Tucson Tabernacle Books), p. 194.
[9]Green, ibid., p. 196.

Conclusions

Something strange happened at Jonestown, Guyana. People described years before as honest, law-abiding citizens not only murdered others but willingly took their own lives. How was it possible? After all, they grew up in a culture that valued life.

But the People's Temple is not unique. Rabbi Maurice David found that 35 of 90 former Unification church members he had interviewed told him that "if told to kill, they would, whether it was in name of God or man."[10]

Men do not kill, because the law and the Bible say it is wrong. They are our authority, the basis for our conduct. But the people at Jonestown had no law greater than the law of their leader. They used no Bible to teach that killing was wrong. Their new authority demanded unconditional obedience and they unconditionally obeyed to the death.

---

[10]William Ringle, Gannet News Service, printed in the *Herald Dispatch*, Huntington, W. Va., Feb. 20, 1976.

◆ 12 ◆

Building on Quicksand: Washed-Out Truth

The most frequent response I hear from Christians after they discover that a group is a cult is, "But they use and study the Bible so much!" Just because someone uses Scripture does not mean they use it correctly. The Bible is our final authority, but only if we use it properly.

Paul challenged Timothy: "Do your best to present yourself to God as one approved, a workman who does not need to be ashamed and who *correctly* handles the word of truth" (2 Tim. 2:15). Timothy was to interpret with integrity. Paul recognized that the Bible is true only when properly understood.

Many Christians are frustrated with God and bitter against Christianity because they misunderstood a promise of God. With great faith, they stepped out on a limb only to have the limb chopped off and their faith crushed. Why? Because they crawled out on the *wrong* limb. God is worthy of trust and He keeps His promises; but misreading the Bible causes misunderstandings.

Interpreting Scripture can be very difficult. We try to express what the biblical authors meant. Because it seems that so much is based on personal opinion, we often avoid judging other interpretations. After all, who can say that someone else is wrong and that I am right. The Bible may be inerrant, but none of us are.

However, does interpretation need to be so subjective? Are there rules which can help us? The Bible has been given to us with the intent that we could read it, understand it, and apply it. There are some definite principles of interpretation. When these rules are broken, doctrine goes askew.

Revelation and Interpretation

God inspired the authors of Scripture to communicate specific truth. We call this truth *revelation*. God communicated His revelation in human language, and human language is adequate to communicate those things which He chose to reveal. We can comprehend Scripture just as God intended. Since it is written, we use the rules of language, definitions, grammar, and syntax to understand it, not just hunches.

Mysteries are truths that God did not fully reveal to us. They are not truths hidden within the text. Scripture is revelation and that which God chose to conceal was not written (Dan. 12:4).

Some might contend that parables are mysteries, but they are understood on the basis of language rules or clarified with further revelation. There are no mysteries veiled in the written words that can be discerned only by prophets with spiritual intuition. What is there is there for all.

Illumination is the work of the Holy Spirit, helping the reader understand more clearly or apply more specifically the truth revealed in the words of the Bible. Illumination does not explain mysteries hidden in the text. It clarifies the author's intent.

The term "revelation" often is used when the term "illumination" should be. A believer will stand up in church and rave about a *revelation* he received from God when the Spirit had actually given him *illumination*. This can be misleading. Young Christians who hear this may become susceptible to similar statements by cultists. I am very uncomfortable with people who say that God revealed anything to them.

Many claims of "revelations from God" contradict what has already been revealed. Even if one is not contradictory, it is not necessarily a true revelation from God. The danger in giving our opinions more authority than they really have by calling them revelations is that our disciples may not be able to discern the danger signal when a cultist says the same thing.

Illumination interprets revelation. There is generally one correct interpretation, one meaning, for any scripture. If there are two, then both cannot be correct. Both may be wrong, but a maximum of one can be true. If the author's intent is clear, then the passage interprets itself. Determining the full and exact meaning of the biblical author is the interpreter's task.

Although there is one meaning, the Spirit may demonstrate a variety of different applications. However, an application is not an interpretation.

Notice that I said that there is generally one meaning. I qualified my statement because I cannot simply say an author did not intentionally use plays on words. If the author did, the language and context will point to that. It will not be a secret message for elite prophets.

Other books deal with biblical puns. You only need to know that double meanings are the exception, not the rule. Therefore, the advocate of any exception must give a biblical basis for the exception. If a group consistently claims dual meanings in Scripture be very careful.

Existential Interpretation

An *existential interpretation* is based upon personal intuition or feelings, not on words, grammar, or syntax. Some call it *esoteric interpretation*.

A cult may alter Scripture's intent by claiming a deeper hidden meaning or existential interpretation that is understood by its prophets or teachers. William Marrion Branham exemplifies this:

> Bringing these two thoughts together you will see that it won't take just ordinary study and thinking to make this Book real. It is going to take the operation of the Holy Ghost. That means this Book can't be revealed to anyone but a special class of people. It will take one with prophetic insight. It will require the ability to hear from God. It will require supernatural instruction, not just a student comparing verse with verse, though that is good. But a mystery requires the teaching of the Spirit or it never becomes clear.[1]

The idea often proposed is that there are various levels of meaning. Christians may be correct on one level but miss a "spiritual meaning."

---

[1]William Marrion Branham, *An Exposition of the Seven Church Ages* (Tucson, Ariz.), p. 16.

Mary Baker Eddy, in her *Science and Health* uses this technique when she discusses the meaning of Adam in the Garden of Eden.

> Divide the name of Adam into two syllables, and it reads, a dam, or obstruction. This suggests the thought of something fluid, of mortal mind in solution. It further suggests the thought of that "darkness . . . upon the face of the deep," when matter or dust was deemed the agent of Deity in creating man, when matter, as that which is accursed, stood opposed to Spirit. Here a dam is not a mere play upon words; it stands for obstruction, error, even the supposed separation of man from God, and the obstacle which the serpent, sin, would impose between man and his creator.[2]

James Sire, in discussing this method in his book *Scripture Twisting*, makes a good observation.

> Suddenly the writer had turned from the Hebrew to the English and developed an exegesis based on a pun. This is such an obvious misreading that I might not have used this passage as an example had it not derived from a major text from a major cult.[3]

Do you think Moses knew enough English to plan this idea? Yet, this method is typical of Eddy's writing.

> The Scriptures are very sacred. Our aim must be to have them understood spiritually, for only by this understanding can truth be gained.[4]

Ultimately, existential interpretation destroys any basis for truth. The Bible remains an inerrant authority, but if the author's words are not the real meaning of the text, then we have dissolved their authority. The Apostle Paul says one thing, Mary Baker Eddy says another, and Herbert W. Armstrong says something else. All discuss the same verse but derive different meanings. Who is right? If there are several meanings, then Paul's opinion carries no more weight than anyone else's.

First Corinthians, chapter two, is particularly confusing in relationship to existential interpretation. Some have used it to

---

[2]Mary Baker Eddy, *Science and Health with Key to the Scriptures* (Boston, Mass.: The First Church of Christ, Scientist, 1971), p. 338.

[3]James Sire, *Scripture Twisting* (Downers Grove, Ill.: InterVarsity Press, 1980), p. 65.

[4]Mary Baker Eddy, *Science and Health with Key to the Scriptures* (Boston, Mass.: The First Church of Christ, Scientist, 1971), p. 547.

justify their search for hidden meanings.

> No, we speak of God's secret wisdom, a wisdom that has been hidden and that God destined for our glory before time began. But God has revealed it to us by his Spirit. The Spirit searches all things, even the deep things of God. We have not received the spirit of the world but the Spirit who is from God, that we may understand what God has freely given us. This is what we speak, not in words taught us by human wisdom but in words taught by the Spirit, expressing spiritual truths in spiritual words. The man without the Spirit does not accept the things that come from the Spirit of God, for they are foolishness to him, and he cannot understand them, because they are spiritually discerned. (1 Cor. 2:7, 10, 12–14)

Paul appears to say that there is special wisdom and knowledge given by the Spirit only to Christians. Non-Christians are unable to perceive these spiritual truths.

But does this passage teach that Christians, because they are indwelt by the Holy Spirit, have the ability to perceive hidden truths in the Bible? If we place these verses in context and define some of the terms, we will see that is not true.

Paul begins this discussion in 1 Cor. 1:17. There he says that he did not come to baptize "but to preach the gospel—not with words of human wisdom, lest the cross of Christ be emptied of its power." This entire section of Scripture revolves around the mystery of Jesus Christ and the cross, how man responds to the mystery, and the work of the Spirit in helping man respond.

What is the mystery? Paul begins by defining it, and continues to declare it. It is that Jesus, the Lord of Glory, was crucified for our sins (1:18, 21, 23, 24, 30; 2:2; see also Col. 2:1–3). The mystery is not a veiled secret available only to spiritual people. This is God's wisdom. It was a mystery, but it has been revealed (2:7–8). Man's wisdom did not bring men to God. Man's wisdom considered God's wisdom foolish.

Therefore, Paul did not depend upon man's wisdom or persuasive words when he preached at Corinth. Yet, as Paul says, the rulers of this age did not understand God's wisdom, for if they had, they would not have crucified the Lord of Glory (2:7–8). Mankind had been told about the wisdom of God, but they only understand it in an intellectual way. They never grasped the spiritual import.

What seems to be the difference between those who accept God's wisdom as the power of God and those who reject it as foolishness? The difference is the work of the Holy Spirit. God calls them. Paul said, "It is because of him that you are in Christ Jesus, who has become for us wisdom from God" (1 Cor. 1:30).

This is why Paul did not depend upon human wisdom to communicate the gospel, but on the powerful work of the Spirit.

> My message and my preaching were not persuasive words of wisdom, but in demonstration of the Spirit and of power, that your faith should not rest on the wisdom of men, but on the power of God. (1 Cor. 2:4–5)

Quite naturally, we who have the Spirit of God understand the wisdom of God. The natural man does not understand or accept it (1 Cor. 2:14).

Jesus Christ crucified was foolishness to the unregenerate. The Spirit's work helps us accept this wisdom. Paul, as an apostle, was given not only the mystery of salvation and Christ but other mysteries, too. He wrote them for us in his epistles. These are not hidden between the lines of Scripture, they *are* the Scriptures.

The Error of Scripture Out of Context

I have never been to a baby shower, but I have heard rumors of what goes on. Sure, it sounds safe and clean. After all, it's called a *shower*. It may begin with tasty little hors d'oeuvres, punch, cookies, and presents; but sooner or later it's bound to happen, as inevitable as winter after fall, as pain after jogging, or tests after semesters: The hostess pulls out the word games. "In three minutes," she explains, "see how many words you can get out of the word *maternity*" or "Unscramble these letters and find words that refer to babies."

However, we do not play word games to better understand the Bible. Cults do this and wind up with a crop of twisted truths. Their favorite game is to play with the context of words and verses in Scripture.

Every word is part of a verse and every verse is part of a book. A verse is not independent from the verses around it. The authors of Scripture wrote sentence after sentence, never stopping to divide their work into chapters and verses. The verses are not a list of thousands of unrelated little ideas or profound magical truisms.

Verses are often parts of a paragraph attempting to communicate a main idea. Sentences and clauses are grouped to explain, expand, or develop the main idea of the paragraph. Some sentence construction further explains the main idea by illustrating it or quoting other scriptural evidence. However, each sentence and verse is part of an uninterrupted context.

When you attempt to understand a word, it is best defined by the words in its context. There are several spheres of context, but the inner spheres can most accurately give the meaning of the word or phrase in question. Besides that, you may use the word or phrase in larger and more expanding contexts. These spheres unlock the shades of meaning of each word.

Spheres of Context

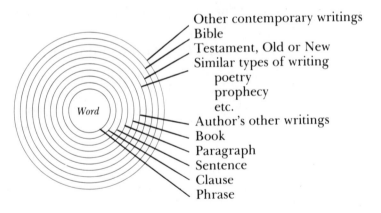

Other contemporary writings
Bible
Testament, Old or New
Similar types of writing
    poetry
    prophecy
    etc.
Author's other writings
Book
Paragraph
Sentence
Clause
Phrase

Word

Ignoring Context

To ignore context is to create errors. There are several types of contextual errors that cultists may use. The first is *ignoring the surrounding context*. This is done by quoting only a part of a verse and letting it imply something different than the author intended. But words, phrases, clauses, and sentences are glued together to form a paragraph. Ripping a portion out is like removing one leg from a three-legged stool; it changes the meaning and purpose drastically.

Thus, it is very important, when evaluating someone's use of Scripture, to look up the text and see how it relates to the paragraph in which it is located. Always check out the verse in its context.

The Mormon pamphlet *The Plan of Salvation* contends that Jesus will preach to the dead, offering them a second chance. One of the proof texts it cites is 1 Cor. 15:19:

> Paul beautifully and aptly expressed the principle in writing to the Corinthians: "If in this life only we have hope in Christ, we are of all men most miserable," (1 Cor. 15:19) but knowing that the gospel would be preached to the spirits in prison, and that untold millions of those who failed to accept the gospel here would do so there, he felt to rejoice in his heart instead of being the most miserable of men.[5]

Is Paul saying that he is not miserable because he knows people will have another chance after death? Read the verse in context.

> More than that, we are then found to be false witnesses about God, for we have testified about God that he raised Christ from the dead. But he did not raise him if in fact the dead are not raised. For if the dead are not raised, then Christ has not been raised either. And if Christ has not been raised, your faith is futile; you are still in your sins. Then those who have fallen asleep in Christ are lost. If only for this life we have hope in Christ, we are to be pitied more than all men. (1 Cor. 15:15–19)

The context is clear. Paul is developing a case to prove resurrection from the dead. He uses Jesus as an example. If Christ has not been raised from the dead, then there is no salvation. If there is no salvation, we have hope in Christ only in this life, false hope. Moreover, those Christians who have already died never obtained salvation. They are still in their sins, and worthy of pity.

Another example of stealing a verse out of its context is found in Mary Baker Eddy's *Science and Health*. She concludes one of

---

[5]*The Plan of Salvation*, p. 24, Mormon Pamphlet.

her chapters quoting John 14:16:

> In the words of St. John: "He shall give you another Comforter, that he may abide with you forever," This Comforter I understand to be Divine Science.[6]

But what does John 14:16 say in its context?

> And I will ask the Father, and he will give you another Counselor to be with you forever—the Spirit of truth. The world cannot accept him, because it neither sees him nor knows him. But you know him, for he lives with you and will be in you. (John 14:16–17)

The comforter is the Holy Spirit. This becomes even clearer as Jesus continues in John 16:7–16.

Victor Paul Wierwille also ignores context. He does not believe Jesus is God but that He first existed when he was born of Mary in Bethlehem. Before that, he was a twinkle in God's eye, existing only in His foreknowledge.

The first chapter of Colossians says Jesus was the preexisting creator of all things. How does Wierwille deal with this passage? He actually deletes two verses from the context. He writes:

> Verse 16 and 17 of Colossians 1 form a parenthesis which is a figure of speech explaining in more detail one point in the text. When a parenthesis is employed, one must proceed in reading from the last word preceding the parenthesis to the first word after the parenthesis. No thought continuity is lost, and the truth is quickly evident.

> Reading from the last word of verse 15 directly on to verse 18 without reading the parenthesis of verse 16 and 17 will give the following statement:
> > Who (Jesus Christ) is the image of the invisible God, the firstborn of every creature.
> > And (Jesus Christ) is the head of the body, the church. . . .
> > the parenthetical verses 16 and 17 refer to what God did.[7]

I hope you caught what he did. Verses 16 and 17 declare that Christ created the world, so Wierwille says, "Skip 'em, then come

---

[6]Mary Baker Eddy, *Science and Health with Key to the Scriptures* (Boston, Mass.: The First Church of Christ, Scientist, 1971), p. 55.

[7]Victor Paul Wierwille, *Jesus Christ is not God* (New Knoxville, Ohio: American Christian Press, 1981), p. 120.

back and read God (in reference to the Father), not Jesus, back into them." It might seem possible because of the period at the end of the sentence in verse 15. However, the Greek text has no period. It reveals a series of clauses introduced with pronouns, all of which refer back to and describe the antecedent, the Son. This includes verse 16 and 17. The Son created the world and sustains it.

Sometimes context runs deeper than just the paragraph in which the word is found. The context may include the whole chapter or entire book.

Quite ironically, this can be seen in the Mormon's use of Paul's warning to the Galatians against perverting the gospel (Gal. 1:7–8). It is not until we get to Gal. 2:16 that Paul finally tells us what evil he is so concerned about: works salvation.

> Know that a man is not justified by observing the law, but by faith in Jesus Christ. So we, too, have put our faith in Christ and not by observing the law, because by observing the law, no one will be justified.

Nevertheless, notice how the Mormons twist this warning:

> Paul writing to the Galatians, speaks of those who were "perverting" the gospel; doubtless teaching such things as that the laying on of hands was not necessary, or else that it was done away with, and says, "But though we, or an angel from heaven, preach any other gospel unto you than that which we have preached unto you, let him be accursed." (Galatians 1:8)[8]

Mormons contend that the laying on of hands is one of the necessary steps for salvation. Doubtless they should have laid their hands on a New Testament that included Galatians, chapter 2.

Creating False Context

A second type of contextual error is combining phrases or verses from different contexts that have little or no relationship to each other. It's the perfect way to create incorrect conclusions. If we were allowed to take phrases and verses from various passages and paste them together with no regard for context, we could create any doctrine we wished.

---

[8]*The Plan of Salvation*, p. 15, Mormon Pamphlet.

I once heard a radio preacher use this technique with four separate verses. Jesus prophesied that He would rise from the dead on the third day (John 2:19). This was to be a bodily resurrection (John 2:21). The Church is called the body of Christ (1 Cor. 12:12). Since a day is as a thousand years (2 Pet. 3:8), the church will be raptured (resurrected) in the third millennium, after the year 2,000.

In combining verses, we must ask if there is a relationship between the different sections. Are they discussing the same issue and are they relevant to each other?

Another version of combining verses is to take a single word and collect verses using that word. In many cases this results in good doctrine, but only if the context makes it clear the word means the same thing in every passage. If we use passages in which the word has different meanings, we wind up with heresy like this: The word *world* has many meanings. In first John it says, "Do not love the *world* or anything in the *world*. If anyone loves the *world*, the love of the Father is not in him" (1 John 2:15). But the same author says that "God so loved the *world*" (John 3:16). Does God do what He forbids?

Paul says "those who are in the *flesh* cannot please God" (Rom. 8:8, NASB). Yet John says that "the Word became *flesh*" (John 1:14). Was Jesus displeasing to God? Of course not. The first verse refers to man's sinful bent and the second to a physical body. How do we know? Because the contexts clearly say so.

The Jehovah's Witnesses create a false context in discussing Jesus' promise of paradise to the forgiven thief on the cross (Luke 23:43). Their problem is that they believe only tested, faithful Christians go to heaven; the rest will live in paradise on earth in the future.[9] Therefore, they explain:

> But what does Jesus mean when he says: "You will be with me in Paradise"? Where is Paradise? Well, where was the paradise God made at the beginning? It was on earth, was it not? God put the first human pair in the beautiful paradise called the garden of Eden. So when we read that this former criminal will be in Paradise, we should picture in our minds this earth made

---

[9]*You Can Live Forever in Paradise on Earth* (New York: Watchtower Bible and Tract Society of New York, Inc., 1982), p. 124.

into a beautiful place in which to live, for the word "paradise" means "garden" or "park."[10]

Was Jesus talking about living on earth in some future millennium, or in heaven with Him that day? Context makes the answer clear. Jesus said it would be *today*, knowing they were both near death.

Rewriting Text

While some cults take scripture out of context, some simply alter the text itself. Generally, this is the motivation for those groups that develop their own translations of the Bible. The Jehovah's Witnesses *New World Translation* (NWT) is a hybrid of additions, deletions, and mutations of the original. Explanatory words dot the text. For example, Col. 1:15–16 in the NWT reads:

15 He is the image of the invisible God, the first born of all creation;

16 because by means of him all (other) things were created . . .

Joseph Smith also attempted to complete a new, improved translation of the Bible. He added to the text to protect his doctrines.

No Man has seen God at any time, (except them who believe). If we love one another, God dwells in us, and His love is perfected in us. (1 John 4:12)[11]

The Error of Redefinition

Redefinition is simply taking a word or concept and giving it another meaning. If we were allowed to redefine terms, our doctrine might differ from the intents of biblical authors. Recall our chapter on discussing the Son of God. Most cults believe Jesus is the Son of God, but they have given new definitions to that concept. Redefinition is often used to deceive possible converts into thinking the cult is orthodox by using familiar terms.

Christian Scientists seek the deeper meanings of the words of the Bible. Therefore, they redefine many terms. "Atonement,"

---

[10]*You Can Live Forever in Paradise on Earth*, ibid., p. 170.
[11]Walter Martin, *Mormonism* (Minneapolis, Minn.: Bethany House Publishers, 1957), p. 28.

rather than being the sacrifice of Christ on the cross for our sins, is "at-one-ment," or "at harmony with God." *Science and Health* constantly reinterprets scriptural terms and principles. An example of the *Science and Health* version of the Lord's prayer will suffice.

> Here let me give what I understand to be the spiritual sense of the Lord's prayer:
>
> Our Father which art in heaven,
>> Our Father-Mother God, all harmonious,
>
> Hallowed be Thy name.
>> Adorable One.
>
> Thy kingdom come.
>> Thy kingdom is come; Thou art ever-present.
>
> Thy will be done in earth, as it is in heaven.
>> Enable us to know,—as in heaven, so on earth,
>> —God is omnipotent, supreme.
>
> Give us this day our daily bread;
>> Give us grace for to-day; feed the famished
>> affections;
>
> And forgive us our debts, as we forgive our debtors.
>> And Love is reflected in love;
>
> And lead us not into temptation, but deliver us from evil;
>> And God leadeth us not into temptation, but delivereth us
>> from sin, disease, and death.
>
> For Thine is the kingdom, and the power, and the glory, forever.
>> For God is infinite, all-power, all Life, Truth,
>> Love, over all, and All.[12]

Christian Science obviously redefines. However, other cults are more subtle.

Mormon theology is not comfortable with everlasting punishment. Mormons believe Christ preaches salvation to those who have died without hearing the gospel. Those who repent can advance. The rest will be annihilated. Naturally the doctrine of eternal punishment needs redefining to harmonize. Thus, they say:

> We hear the question asked, "Do not the scriptures say that it is

---

[12]Mary Baker Eddy, *Science and Health with Key to the Scriptures* (Boston, Mass.: The First Church of Christ, Scientist, 1971), p. 16–17.

'eternal punishment' and 'everlasting punishment'?" We answer, "Yes." But let us not put any private interpretations on these terms, but correctly understand their meaning.

Eternal punishment is God's punishment; everlasting pun- ishment is God's punishment; or in other words, it is the name of the punishment God inflicts, he being eternal in His nature.[13]

God is eternal, but the meaning of "eternal" must be defined by the context where it is used. Eternal describes the duration of the punishment. It generally means "a very, very, very long time" or "forever." "Eternal" also describes God as being "forever." However, there is no reason to make the attribute "eternal" mean "God." Punishment is never described by God's other attributes. It is never omnipotent, omnipresent, immutable, or benevolent punishment. It is called *eternal punishment* because the punish- ment lasts forever.

Changing the meaning of words or phrases is like taking the wrong road—you end up a good distance from your proper des- tination. Be careful of the man who says, "This really means . . ." Do not criticize the good expositional preacher who provides synonyms for biblical word studies, but check these definitions out if he takes you down new doctrinal paths. Ask yourself, "With all the good translations today, why didn't anyone translate it this way?"

We must admit that some words or concepts defy definition. This is why cultists love the symbols, prophetic passages, para- bles, figures of speech, and poetic devices in the Bible. Distinct meaning in these styles of literature is elusive and Christians are often hesitant to challenge their interpretations. Nevertheless, these literary devices do exist, so we need to study them to as- certain the meaning in the mind of the author.

David Moses, the leader of the Children of God, quotes Jesus as saying that "you must hate your parents" (Luke 14:26). He has ignored the figure of speech called *hyperbole*, the deliberate exaggeration of an idea to make a point. Jesus was stressing the need for unreserved commitment to the kingdom of God over all family ties. He spoke of choosing priorities in terms of *loving*

---

[13]*The Plan of Salvation*, p. 30, Mormon Pamphlet.

and *hating*. Yet, misunderstanding it causes considerable difficulty.

Symbolism can also be a source of problems if we try to use it to prove doctrinal points. The dew on Gideon's fleece was probably water and not a symbol of baptismal regeneration or the Holy Spirit. Jeremiah 10 in the KJV does not describe Christmas trees. When the authors used the symbols, they had a purpose. Do we really believe that Jeremiah wanted to warn his audience of the potential danger of Christmas trees in the future twentieth century? More likely, he was describing the practice of making idols in his own time.

The Error of Selective Biblicity

The entire Bible is the revelation of God. It is the responsibility of the interpreter to find harmony in Scripture. An interpretation of one section cannot be correct if it contradicts other clear revelation. Scripture interprets itself.

Cults consistently ignore the sections of Scripture that contradict their doctrines. They use the Bible selectively. If they desire to promote legalism, they ignore grace passages. If they desire submission, they emphasize passages on authority.

Be careful on the one-book emphasis. A group that emphasizes *Deuteronomy* to the exclusion of others will develop a legalistic flavor. *The Psalms* lead to worship, but lack of doctrinal depth in many areas. *Revelation* may be exciting, but if we study it exclusively, we will not understand how to live as a Christian on a daily basis.

Conclusion

I am not attempting to create church members who are critical, but critical thinkers. Never be ashamed to ask questions. See what the Bible says for yourself. When someone uses a verse to prove a point ask, "Does this verse really say what he claims it says? Or must I read something into the verse to get his conclusion? What is the relationship of this verse to its context? How does it relate to the rest of the Bible? Is he redefining words in the text? Is he combining several verses with no relationship to each other? Does his conclusion contradict other clear scripture? The Bible, to be a good authority, must be handled correctly.

◆ 13 ◆

Back to the Basics

Doctrinal Balance

There are two views of doctrine that are extremes. The first claims that doctrine is unimportant. In some cases, this is due to the fact that experience has become more important than doctrine.

But more often today, doctrine is devalued because some feel the Bible is unreliable. Therefore, doctrinal positions based upon the Bible do not carry authority. Doctrine begins to resemble the teachings of cults. Nonnegotiable biblical tenets are sacrificed for the sake of a false unity. Ironically, this camp strongly urges unity but denies the true basis of unity.

The other extreme elevates nearly every possible doctrine, tradition, and nuance to the level of nonnegotiable truth. Unless we hold to their entire long list of infallible interpretations, there can be absolutely no fellowship. The first extreme promotes cultic doctrines and this extreme promotes cultic practices. It breeds isolation, guilt manipulation, fear, strong authoritarian control, and the restriction of free thought expression.

Of course we can elevate any minor doctrine to the level of a nonnegotiable absolute. We all have practice at that. How many husbands and wives have fought about where to squeeze the toothpaste tube, claiming that they were arguing a *deeper principle*. In marriages, the real principle is often pride. I have a feeling that the same is true in theology.

As members of the church, we need to define those areas which are set in cement and hold tightly to them. The issues in this book define what I feel are some of those nonnegotiables.

There are more, but most of what the church wrestles over is not.

Before we can reach out to the world, we must clean our own house. We need to reaffirm our basic beliefs, set aside any issues that divide us, and begin to work together.

An Effective Mission

If God has revealed himself in the Scriptures (and He has), then there is only one name under heaven by which man can be saved. We are ambassadors with the ministry of reconciliation. Many people involved in cults are there because the cults have met their needs for love, acceptance, purpose, a place to belong, or just being needed. But the greatest need of all is salvation. Jesus can certainly meet all these needs better than some guru, especially the need for forgiveness. As representatives of Christ, we need to reach out to people and meet those needs.

Cultists are tied to their own value systems. They are often held by strong authoritarian control. Emotional manipulation is used to keep them isolated and committed to the group. Teaching fear of other "devilish" perspectives keeps them. Like a person holding on to a life preserver, they clutch tighter the more you attempt to pull them away. Only when they see that they must release the life preserver to be pulled into the boat will they let go. Cults teach that they are the only life preserver, that the rescuers are really enemies. Until their fears are minimized and they see their needs met by Christians, they will be hesitant to listen to the church.

Therefore, the Christian apologist may need *more* than sound biblical arguments. Actions of assistance may open the door for them to see the alternative of the gospel of Christ. Once the instilled fears of a false prophet are recognized, the cultist will more likely listen to the church.

Nevertheless, apologetics is important. One young Jehovah's Witness feared that her faith was destroying her marriage. She wanted to be free, and yet feared leaving the "only way to salvation," and the "only ones who had the truth." When she finally saw that the Jehovah's Witnesses were false prophets, she leaped for liberty in Christ. Her barrier, the fear of leaving what she had believed was the truth, had finally been broken down. "Then you will know the truth, and the truth will set you free" (John 8:32).

Study Questions for Part IV

1. What is authority?
2. How does authority govern our lives?
3. How do cults use authority?
4. How do cults shift authority?
5. What is the authority for Christian faith?
6. Is the Bible a reliable authority?
7. How do cults alter biblical authority?
8. What tests does the Bible give for false prophets?
9. If a group uses the Bible, does it mean that they are not a cult?
10. How do cults twist the Scriptures?
11. What is an existential interpretation?
12. Why is an existential interpretation wrong?
13. How many meanings can a scripture passage have?
14. What is revelation?
15. What is illumination?
16. How do cults misuse context?
17. What is cultic redefinition of terms?
18. What is the error of selective biblicity?

✦ Appendix A ✦

John 8:58

"I tell you the truth," Jesus answered, "before Abraham was born, I am!"

The clause "I am" (*ego eimi*) is a present-tense form of the verb "to be" describing a quality of Jesus' existence. In Greek, the present tense describes a continuous action. "To be" means one who continues to be or exist. On the other hand, an aorist (or simple past) tense in Greek, describes Abraham's existence. He "came into being." When we see the aorist with the verb it implies birth. The point is clear, before Abraham was born, or came into being, Jesus continually existed.

The distinction is explained more by Raymond Brown when he says that "was born" (*egenomein*) is used of mortals while "to be" (*eimi*) is used of the divine. He says, "The same distinction was seen in the prologue, the Word *was*, but through him all things *came into being*. In the Old Testament Septuagint, the same distinction is found in the address to Yahweh in Ps. XC2:1 'Before the mountains *came into being* . . . from age to age you *are*!' "[1]

If John wanted to say that Jesus simply existed before Abraham, he would have used *heimein* or *egenomein*, an aorist tense implying that Jesus was born or came into existence just as Abraham, but at an earlier date.

The Jehovah's Witnesses have spent considerable time in altering this verse. They respond that "I have been" (*ego eimi*) follows the aorist infinitive clause "before Abraham was born" (*prin*

---

[1] Raymond Brown, *The Gospel According to St. John*, p. 360.

Abraam genesthai) and hence is properly rendered in the perfect tense.[2] The answer sounds good, but means very little.

Another Jehovah's Witness response is to appeal to other "I am" statements in the New Testament, attempting to demonstrate that "I am" (*ego eimi*) in John 8:58 is neither unique nor significant. However, the "I am" of John 8:58 is used in the *absolute* way, that is, without predicate or modifiers. This usage is not common and is, therefore, very important.

Within certain circles a widely held view about this "I am" is that Jesus' claim to deity was clear because He quoted the Septuagint from Ex. 3:14 and applied the divine name to himself. It is a very simple and powerful explanation of John 8:58 that is popular with a vast number of individuals.

But as with many simple and powerful arguments, more study indicates that the issue is much more complex than anticipated. For example, one who possesses a copy of the Septuagint may turn to Ex. 3:14 and find that an argument by the Jehovah's Witnesses appears more valid than they desire!

Ex. 3:14 says:

> God said to Moses, "I am who I am (*ego eimi ho on*). This is what you are to say to the Israelites: 'I AM (*ho on*) has sent me to you.'"

The contention made by the Jehovah's Witnesses appears valid. It seems that the divine name is really *ho on*, not *ego eimi*. They are wrong, but even so, you scurry as I did, to find textual variations in other editions of the Septuagint. Unfortunately, they all agree. The simple has turned quite complex.

Hebrew names communicate character and description. Both "I am" (*ego eimi*) and "who I am" (*ho on*) are equivalent in that purpose. Both communicate eternality of being. Hebrew and Greek are distinctly different. The men who translated the Greek Septuagint from the Hebrew had to find a means of communicating the intent of the Hebrew into the Greek style. There are three elements of the divine name used in Ex. 3:14 in the Hebrew. For sake of clarity, I will identify them as A, B, and A'. The

---

[2]*Kingdom Interlinear Translation of the Gospel Scriptures* (New York: Watchtower Bible & Tract Society of Pennsylvania, 1969), p. 467.

third element is A' because it is the same word as A.

I am	who	I am
A	B	A'

In Ex. 3:14 only one element is used, either A or A'. It does not matter which. Both are equal.

When the translators put the divine name into Greek, they chose to use only two elements. They combined B and A' into one element, *ho on*.

I am	that I am
A	B
ego eimi	*ho on*

In the Septuagint, A is a pronoun and a verb. The verb, because it is in the present tense, communicates continual existence, just as in John 8:58. But element B is a participle, a verb used as a noun. Here it has its own definite article. Even though it is a noun in usage, it still communicates the exact meaning of element A.

Element B is used in Ex. 3:14 because a verbal element, "has sent," is already present. Therefore, a noun element, not another verbal element, is required. Since element B is nominal and element A is verbal, element B was chosen. Remember, they communicate the same character and nature.

Because of this problem, others have suggested that Jesus quoted the Septuagint from either Deut. 32:39, Joel 2:27, Hosea 13:4, or Isaiah, rather than from Exodus. In Isaiah "I am" is used in reference to God seven times (41:4; 43:10–13; 44:6; 45:18, 21; 46:4; 48:12).

Again we turn in our copies of the Septuagint and another problem surfaces. The Greek constructions in several of the passages are not attributive, but predicative. This means that *ego eimi* is followed by a predicate noun or a predicate adjective. Now remember, in John 8:58 the Jehovah's Witnesses contend that *ego eimi* is not unique but that it refers to a number of places where the phrase is followed by a predicate nominative or adjective. As we said, the strength of John 8:58 is that the construction is attributive and not predicative. But suddenly we find ourselves appealing to several predicative constructions in Isaiah. In order to preserve what may be becoming an exegetical "sacred cow," we may be undermining the power of John 8:58. This is another reason some feel that Jesus could not be quoting from Ex. 3:14. The construction there is predicative also.

Other passages must supply the "am" (*eimi*) because it does not exist in the text. However, there are some passages which do use *ego eimi* in the attributive fashion.

We are certain that God communicated His divine name in the Old Testament, a name which declared His eternality. But we cannot be certain that Jesus was quoting the Septuagint, if indeed He did, where He quoted from.

Here is how I view John 8:58. Even though Jesus, being the Son of God, probably knew Greek, just as many of the Jews did, He was most likely speaking to the Pharisees in Aramaic, their native language. During the conversation, He applied the divine name to himself. They clearly understood His intent, for they picked up stones with which to kill Him.

Along comes John, writing his gospel in Greek. He encountered the same problem that the translators of the Septuagint had in accurately communicating the Semitic meaning into the Greek. He might have drawn from his knowledge of that Greek version of the Scriptures, or he might not have. It really does not matter because the translation stands strongly upon its own merits within the context.

The point is this, we should not spend all our energy attempting to prove Jesus quoted from the Septuagint. That is not the most important issue. Some seem more concerned with defending the position that Jesus "quoted," rather than letting the statement of Jesus speak for itself.

John 8:58 makes it very clear that Jesus claimed deity. Let's spend our energy defending that. The issue is not what Jesus quoted, but what He said.

⬩ Appendix B ⬩

Hebrews 1:8

But about the Son he says, "Your throne, O God, will last for ever and ever, and righteousness will be the scepter of your kingdom.

Jehovah's Witnesses and the Way International appeal to another syntactically possible translation. "Thy throne is God (or divine) forever and ever." This alternative is possible because the Greek has no verb "is"; it must be supplied by the translator. This is not unusual.

But where do we supply the verb? Do we translate the clause, "Thy throne, O God, is forever and ever," or "Thy throne is God forever"? The cultist, wishing to deny the deity of the Son opts for the second alternative. Can we decide which translation is better without flipping a quarter?

Fortunately, the Hebrews passage is a quote from another source. The original source, Ps. 45:6, although the Hebrew is not easily translated, does shift the scales to the first translation. In Hebrew, we still have to provide the "to be," but we have other factors that help us know where to place it.

There are three possible translations of this verse. The term for "God" in Hebrew, (*elohim*), can refer to divinity or to judges and rulers. Therefore, the verse is not necessarily addressed to God but to kings. However, the syntax makes this alternative impossible because the suphormative, the pronoun attached to the Hebrew "throne," is singular, not plural.

In Hebrew, pronominal elements or pronouns are often attached to other Hebrew words. If the pronominal element refers to another term, it must agree with it in both number and gender.

In this case, the suphormative "your," which is attached to "throne" and modifies *elohim*, is singular, not plural. Therefore, *elohim* is a singular term and refers to one, God, and not kings.

A second alternative interpretation would place the verb "is" between "throne" and God," making it say, "Your throne is God." This placement of the verb would force the term *elohim* to be translated "divine." This is the alternative the cults use in Heb. 1:8. However, there is no clear passage in the rest of the Old Testament that one could cite to show that *elohim* is used in this way.

This leaves us with the most plausible translation in the Hebrew, "Your throne, O God *elohim* will last for ever and ever."

Wierwille disagrees. He contends that "God" does not necessarily mean the Divine, but a human judge. As proof, Wierwille cites Ps. 82:6, "I said, 'You are "gods"; you are all sons of the Most High.' " This verse out of its context seems to imply that God called many people "God." But looking at the context drastically changes the meaning.

Psalm 82 describes the unrighteous rulers judging partially and wickedly (v. 1–2). These "gods" will themselves be judged by the Great Judge of the earth and will die like men (v. 7–8). If anything, God is using sarcasm to belittle the "mighty leaders."

More important is the use of parallelism in Hebrew poetry. The intent of Hebrew poetry is not to make rhyming jingles, but to use clauses to define each other. Verse 6 contains synonymous parallelism with the second line in apposition to (or clarifying) the first. What does it mean that they are "gods" (*elohim*)? It means that they are "sons of the Most High."

Do the words "sons of God" in this context have the same implication as in Heb. 1:8? Certainly not. In Psalm 82 the rulers hardly had the nature of God! Yet in Hebrews 1, Jesus is the exact representation of God's nature. He is the only begotten Son of God.[1]

---

[1]For further discussion see Archer, *The Encyclopedia of Bible Difficulties* (Grand Rapids, Mich.: Zondervan), p. 374.

• Appendix C •

John 1:1

In the beginning was the Word, and the Word was with God, and the Word was God.

The Jehovah's Witnesses claim that the best translation in verse one is not "God," but "a God." They base this on the fact that there is no definite article in the Greek before "God" (*theos*), making the translation "a God." The definite article in Greek is usually translated "the," but it is also used to give emphasis, or show the relationships of words.

When there is a predicate nominative or predicate adjective, the insertion and deletion of the definite article in Greek simply demonstrates which term is the subject and which term is the predicate adjective or noun. Since "word" (*logos*) has the definite article and "God" (*theos*) does not, "word" is the subject, and "God" is the predicative nominative. Leon Morris offers an interesting insight on the use of the article in this text.

> The true explanation of the absence of the article appears to be given by E.C. Colwell, who has shown that in the New Testament, definite nouns which precede the verb regularly lack the article (FBL, 111, 1983, pp. 12–21). On this verse he comments: "The absence of the article does *not* make the predicate indefinite or qualitative when it precedes the verb; it is indefinite in this position only when the context demands it. The context makes no such demand in the Gospel of John." (op. cit., p. 21)[1]

It seems to me, however, that the purpose of the article with

---

[1]Leon Morris, *Gospel of John, New International Commentary of the New Testament* (Grand Rapids, Mich.: Eerdmans Pub., 1970), p. 77.

the "word" and not "God" demonstrates which term is the subject and which is the predicate nominative. John is using a figure of speech in these verses that depends emphatically upon word order. He uses the word order to express a *climax*.

Nevertheless, he wants "word" to be the subject of the clause in spite of the word order demanded by the climax. Therefore, he places the article with "word" and not "God." Not only does this define "word" as the subject of the clause, but it also maintains the climax and strongly affirms the divinity of "Word." Bullinger, an authority on figures of speech, discusses John 1:1 from this perspective and confirms my contention.

He sees two figures of speech in John 1:1. The first is *hyperbaton*, in which word order is changed to promote emphasis.

> John i.1.—Here the subject, "the Word," being defined by the article which is prefixed to it, can be placed at the end of two of the clauses: "In the beginning was *the Word*, and God *the Word* was": i.e., in plain cold English, "The Word was in the beginning . . . and the Word was God."
>
> The A.V. preserves the *Hyperbaton* in the first clause, but not in the last, because the English idiom will not bear it. But in each case we are to put the stress on "*the Word*."[2]

More importantly, because of the many times "word" (logos) is used, Bullinger sees the entire construction as an *anadiplosis*. Anadiplosis is "the repetition of the same word or words at the end of one sentence and at the beginning of another."[3] "When 'anadiplosis' is repeated in successive sentences, it is called 'climax.' "[4]

He illustrates its application to John 1:1:

> John i.1, 2.—"In the beginning was
> *the Word*: and
> *The Word* was with
> *God*: and
> *God*
>   *the Word* was, and
>   *the same* (word), was in the beginning with God."

---

[2]Bullinger, *Figures of Speech Used in the Bible* (Grand Rapids, Mich.: Baker Book House), p. 694.
[3]Bullinger, ibid., p. 251.
[4]Bullinger, ibid., p. 256.

The order of the words as thus placed in the Greek exhibits, by the figure of *Climax*, a great solemnity in the measured rising of the sense, and emphasizes the fact that "the word was God," for the use of the article in the third proposition preserves the actual sense from being mistaken or hidden by the *Climax*, which is obtained by the inversion of the words from their natural order. Thus, beautifully is the true Deity of the Lord Jesus affirmed.[5]

He again illustrates this pattern in John 1:4–5, affirming that this is the figure of speech John is using:

His attributes and their effect are similarly marked in verses 4 and 5:

John i:4.5.—"In Him was
  life: and the
  life was the
    light of men. And the
    light shineth in
      darkness; and the
      darkness comprehended it not."[6]

"Word" is the subject in all three clauses. If we used an English word order with which we are more familiar, the clauses would read like this:

The Word was in the beginning,
The Word was with God,
The Word was God.
The Same (Word) was in the beginning with God.

---

[5]Bullinger, ibid., p. 257.
[6]Bullinger, ibid., p. 258.

Appendix D

The following rule by Gransville Sharp of a century back still proves to be true: "When the copulative *kai* connects two nouns of the same case, if the article *o* or any of its cases precedes the first of the said nouns or participles, and is not repeated before the second noun or participle, the latter always relates to the same person that is expressed or described by the first noun or participle; i.e., it denotes a farther description of the first-named person.[1]

---

[1]Dana and Mantey, *A Manual Grammar of the Greek New Testament* (New York: MacMillian, 1955), p. 147.